BuriedTreasures
TastyTubers of the World

How to Grow and Enjoy Root Vegetables, Tubers, Rhizomes, and Corms

Beth Hanson
Editor

D0037285

Elizabeth Peters
DIRECTOR OF
PUBLICATIONS

Sigrun Wolff Saphire
SENIOR EDITOR

Mark Tebbitt
SCIENCE EDITOR

Joni Blackburn
COPY EDITOR

Elizabeth Ennis
ART DIRECTOR

Steven Clemants
VICE-PRESIDENT,
SCIENCE &
PUBLICATIONS

Scot Medbury
PRESIDENT

Elizabeth Scholtz
DIRECTOR
EMERITUS

Judith D. Zuk
PRESIDENT
EMERITUS

Handbook #188

Copyright © 2007 by Brooklyn Botanic Garden, Inc.

All-Region Guides, formerly *21st-Century Gardening Series,* are published three times a year at 1000 Washington Ave., Brooklyn, NY 11225.

Subscription included in Brooklyn Botanic Garden subscriber membership dues ($35 per year; $45 outside the United States).

ISBN 13: 978-1-889538-34-1
ISBN 10: 1-889538-34-5

Printed by OGP in China. Printed on recycled paper.

Above: The enormous leaves of giant taro, *Alocasia macrorrhiza,* make a bold statement in a summer border. Cold-climate gardeners dig the tubers of this tropical showstopper in fall— some to cook and eat and some to save for replanting the following spring.

Cover: Originally domesticated in the Andes, potatoes such as this 'Purple Peruvian' have become important food crops in temperate regions around the world.

Buried Treasures:
Tasty Tubers of the World

Tuber Tales

Beth Hanson

What propelled the unassuming spud from its origins on the steep slopes of the Andes to farm fields all over the world? Archaeological evidence uncovered in several spots in South America indicates that people have been eating tubers and roots for many thousands of years. Some ethnobotanists (scientists who study people's agricultural customs) believe that these were among the first plants early peoples cultivated, possibly as long as 10,000 years ago. Our ancestors may have relied on these plants because many tubers and roots can be eaten raw or are simple to prepare and cook—unlike grains. Growers can also propagate tubers and roots vegetatively, easily preserving their desirable traits from one generation to the next.

Over the past millennia, nutritious tubers and roots have traversed the globe with explorers, travelers, and botanists. Thousands of miles from their origins in the Andes, potatoes (*Solanum tuberosum*) now sprout in fields throughout much of the world; yautía or cocoyam (*Xanthosoma sagittifolium*) and taro (*Colocasia esculenta*) traveled from India to the Middle East, Egypt, and the Mediterranean, and from there to Africa and the New World. For millions of people living in the tropics, where cereals and potatoes don't grow, cassava or manioc (*Manihot esculenta*) from South America, sweet potatoes (*Ipomoea batatas*) from the Andes, and yams (*Dioscorea alata*) from eastern Asia are basic staples. And the voyage isn't over yet: Agronomists continue to study many tuber species to determine if they are adaptable to agricultural uses in other regions of the world.

Tubers are nutritious, easy to grow, harvest, and propagate—qualities that have led to the success of plants like taro, *Colocasia esculenta* (foreground), shown at a market in Cairo, Egypt.

Above the water line, flowers and pods of sacred lotus, *Nelumbo nucifera,* make a lovely display in a water garden. The rhizomes below are crisp and moist and can be eaten raw, cooked, or pickled.

Among the 31 plants profiled in the plant encyclopedia starting on page 20, you'll find some familiar species and encounter others that may be new to you. After reading about these you'll surely feel inspired to taste some tubers or try growing a few of the plants in your garden.

Some plants that may already have a home in your garden for their ornamental value rather than their culinary appeal include *Dahlia*, jack-in-the-pulpit (*Arisaema triphyllum*), spring beauty (*Claytonia virginica*), and sacred lotus (*Nelumbo nucifera*). They all have edible underground parts, and all have been part of the diets of people in various parts of the world at various times. These as well as the other tubers in this book will add a new dimension to your vegetable repertoire and will be interesting—and in some cases spectacular-looking—additions to your garden. Use them as foliar accents in your border or plant a few in a container for an unusual display. Read on to learn more about this group of nutritious, fascinating plants.

Corms, Rhizomes, Tubers, Tuberous Roots, and Bulbs

Potatoes and other tubers belong to a group of plants called geophytes, which hoard energy in fleshy underground parts in order to survive unfavorable periods of the year in a semidormant state and fuel rapid growth and reproduction when climatic conditions are right. Cooks and gardeners casually refer to the delicious or merely edible carbohydrate-rich underground storage organs of geophytes as roots and tubers, but botanists prefer a more accurate terminology. They differentiate between corms, rhizomes, tubers, tuberous roots, and bulbs, depending on which part of the plant develops into a fleshy storage organ and what its characteristics are, while recognizing that many of these structures are extremes of a continuum.

Corms are solid, vertical underground stems that usually have a thin outer covering of papery leaves. Each year after flowering, the existing corm is replaced by a new one that develops on top of it. Jack-in-the-pulpit (*Arisaema triphyllum*, page 28) is a corm.

Rhizomes are swollen stems lying horizontally at or below ground level. Sacred lotus (*Nelumbo nucifera*, page 56) grows from a rhizome.

Tubers are the swollen ends of certain underground stems or roots. Yautía (*Xanthosoma sagittifolium*, below and page 82) arises from a tuber. Potatoes (cultivars of *Solanum tuberosum*, pages 72, 95) are also tubers. Earth chestnut (*Lathyrus tuberosus*, page 50) is a tuberous root.

Bulbs are reduced stems bearing modified fleshy leaves and one or more flower buds. Individual bulbs survive for several years and give rise to new bulbs from their disklike basal stems. Not counting kitchen staples garlic and onions, true bulbs are not widely eaten and therefore not covered in this book.

They may look like roots, but most of the underground edibles featured in this book are actually modified stems, including yautía, *Xanthosoma sagittifolium*.

Unearthing the Story of Tubers

James J. Lang

When asked which crops were domesticated first and where, archaeologists used to take a grain-focused approach. After all, the earliest documented crop remains are typically grains, found at ancient sites in dry regions. Samples of primitive einkorn wheat from the arid Near East date back 11,000 to 12,000 years; the region's barley and nonshattering emmer wheats go back 9,000 to 10,000 years. But root crops may have been just as important to early communities.

At Monte Verde in the cool highlands of southern Chile, archaeologists recently found the remains of charred wild potatoes that have been radiocarbon-dated to about 13,000 years ago. The oldest remains for cultivated potatoes, estimated to be 10,0000 years old, have been discovered at sites along the coast in Peru.

Ancient root and tuber remains may be so scarce because they are far more perishable than grains. In addition, many of these plants originated in the wet, humid tropics where organic matter is subject to rapid decay. Not only is the climate of the arid Near East much kinder to plant remains, but hard, dried grains simply last longer than fleshy roots and tubers under most conditions. Finding grain and tuber remains of comparable antiquity is not easy—but not impossible. Some ethnobotanists now believe that roots and tubers were probably the first plants ancient people domesticated, and that they were most likely domesticated in different parts of the world independently.

Taro, *Colocasia esculenta*, has been in cultivation for millennia, moving with people from its native India to warm and humid regions around the world, including Kauai, Hawaii, shown here.

Domesticating Tubers

The dynamics of domestication—the reasons why ancient people favored certain crops—depended on the tools they had to process and cook what they collected in the wild or chose to grow in their gardens. Compared with grains, roots and tubers are easier to grow, propagate, and prepare for eating. Tuber staples like yam (*Dioscorea alata*), taro (*Colocasia esculenta*), giant taro (*Alocasia macrorrhiza*), manioc or cassava (*Manihot esculenta*), yautía or cocoyam (*Xanthosoma sagittifolium*), arrowroot (*Maranta arundinacea*), potato (*Solanum tuberosum*), and sweet potato (*Ipomoea batatas*) are all easy to propagate vegetatively, which greatly simplified their domestication in different parts of the world. Depending on the crop, farmers simply take pieces of vine, stem cuttings, or pieces of root or tuber and replant these to reap a whole new harvest the following growing season. (See "Making More Tubers," page 103, for more information.) In addition, vegetative propagation allows farmers to select roots and tubers for their taste, productivity, or size, with the knowledge that the offspring will turn out exactly the same as the tasty parent plant. By comparison, selecting, drying, and storing seed from growing season to growing season is more work; it requires greater knowledge; and the genetically diverse seed is less likely to produce plants with the same traits as its parents.

People in the Americas first selected and domesticated favored forms of yautía, sweet potato, and manioc in the lowland tropics; their cultivation later spread into

Potato-like in flavor and carbohydrate rich, giant taro, *Alocasia macrorrhiza*, thrives in the heat and humidity of tropical regions, where it is a staple.

Over the course of one growing season, a small tuber of North American native Jerusalem artichoke, *Helianthus tuberosus*, multiplies underground into a sizable crop of nutritious new rhizomes—a feature that endeared tuberous plants like this one to foragers and early farmers.

the highlands. Pacific islanders grew taro—a crop that flourishes in the monsoon rains and probably predates rice cultivation—using irrigation and terracing systems. In Africa, ancient people domesticated yams in the tropical forests and savannas before they grew grains like millet, sorghum, and rice. In southern China, arrowroot and yams were collected along with wild rice.

Just a few starchy taro corms, yams, or potatoes make a good meal. And they are easy to prepare because they don't need a lot of complicated processing first. They can all be roasted over coals or baked over hot stones in makeshift ovens; no special container for boiling is necessary. By contrast, getting a meal from a member of the grass family, which comprises all the cereal grains, is a lot more work. Whether the grain is wild marsh rice or primitive wheat, collectors must cut lots of stalks for each meal and separate the seed heads from the straw. Once the grains are collected and cleaned, they cannot be eaten right away. First, they must be softened, perhaps by soaking them in water. And then they must be boiled, which requires a pot.

Ulluco, *Ullucus tuberosus*, is one of the many crops domesticated by ancient farmers in the Andes, but unlike squashes, potatoes, and peppers, which have been adopted worldwide, it's rarely grown outside South America.

Andean Cornucopia

At the time of the Spanish conquest in the 16th century, Andean farmers had been at work for thousands of years. They cultivated as many different species of plants as cultivated in all of Asia, and more root and tuber crops than any other people on earth, in part because of the region's ecological compression: In the equatorial Andes, to go up or down 3,000 feet is to experience a radical shift in climate and hence in the type of crops that can be produced. What results is a staggering of microclimates up and down the length and breadth of the Andes and a concomitant diversity of plant life. A village in the semitropical lowland yungas is just a couple of days apart by foot from a village high up on the altiplano. Temperate valleys are adjacent to both, just a "step" away.

From this diverse habitat, ancient Andean farmers gathered a unique set of plants for domestication, many of which were unknown in the Old World. The list is long, comprising a great profusion of legumes; squashes; cereal crops such as maize, quinoa, and amaranth; fruits like peppers and tomatoes, pineapples, and papayas; fibers like cotton; and stimulants such as chocolate, vanilla, yerba maté, and coca.

Many of the roots and tubers, such as mauka (*Mirabilis expansa*), and oca (*Oxalis tuberosa*), are still little known and underappreciated outside the Andes. A few, however, were transported around the world and have become staples in many cuisines: sweet potato, cassava (or manioc), and most notably and successfully—the potato.

World-Traveling Potato

The potato's original home is the Lake Titicaca basin in present-day Peru and Bolivia, and it is there that its genetic diversity is greatest. Early farmers promoted this diversity by domesticating eight different potato species.

Since ancient farmers planted multiple types of potatoes together, crosses between them likely occurred spontaneously, when the pollen of one potato pollinated the flowers of another type growing nearby. At harvest time, the ripe fruits—seed balls the size of cherry tomatoes—were scattered. Then, after the rains came, volunteer seedlings came up like weeds in fields left fallow. Any curious farmer who dug up and held over tubers developed from such errant offspring would have created, technically speaking, a new cultivar. Such fortuitous selection interacted with the environment's vertical compression to create the enormous diversity of cultivated potatoes in the Andes.

When the common spud arrived in the Old World, it faced acceptance problems. Aboveground, its foliage was easily confused with Europe's deadly nightshade (*Atropa belladonna*), a plant notorious for its narcotic properties. Guilty by association, the first potatoes

Early farmers were not interested in their potatoes' flowers and seeds but rather in the vegetative action going on underground as cherished tubers made multiples of themselves.

Harvesting tubers, farmers expect no surprises, as the tubers are replicas of the potatoes planted in spring.

were rejected as poisonous and were thought to cause everything from flatulence to leprosy. Cultural prejudices aside, the potato's problems were as much biological as ideological. The first potatoes that reached Spain were from the Andes and adapted to the relatively short days of equatorial latitudes. Transplanted in Europe, they did not set tubers until the fall equinox, in late September, when shorter days prevailed. Unfortunately, in northern Europe, this coincided with foliage-killing early fall frosts, making, the first potatoes unsuited to that region of the world. They did well enough in the south of Spain, however, where potatoes began showing up on the procurement lists of hospitals and monasteries as early as the 1570s.

The potato's greatest success came in Ireland, where it was introduced in the 1580s. The island's cool but frost-free fall gave the crop enough time to mature. By the 1640s, it was already a mainstay of Irish tenant farmers. A century later, it was indispensable. From Ireland, potato cultivation spread across northern Europe as the Andean plant adapted to the long summer days of northern latitudes and suspicion about it abated. By the 1650s, Dutch farmers were growing potatoes; by 1770 the crop was established in Prussia and Poland and by the 1840s in Russia. The potato makes an excellent rotation crop with rye, a staple of northern Europe, because it draws on different soil nutrients and is subject to different pests and diseases than grain crops. It was grown in fields that would otherwise have been left fallow, so farmers added to their food supply without reducing the grain harvest.

Twenty-First-Century Spuds

Today, many Asian countries have turned to the potato for sustenance. Consider China and India, far and away the most populous nations on earth. Between the 1960s and the 1990s, China's potato harvest quadrupled from an average of 12 million metric tons to 48 million a year. That increase made China the world's largest potato producer, far ahead of the Russian Federation's 33 million metric tons. Since then, China's rice harvest has stagnated, but not its potato production, which now exceeds 73 million metric tons.

In India, the potato has found a new niche in the Ganges Valley. Modern rice and wheat varieties mature at least six weeks earlier than older types, allowing time for a potato rotation. Spuds go in during the fall, as nighttime temperatures drop, and are harvested at winter's end. Potato production has surged from just 3 million metric tons in the early 1960s to in excess of 25 million metric tons today.

Sweet Potato Success

Like the potato, the sweet potato (*Ipomoea batatas*) was domesticated in South America, but in the lowlands, on the edge of the Amazon River basin. Even though both crops share a similar common name, they are members of different families and

South American native sweet potato, *Ipomoea batatas*, was transported to Polynesia and beyond in pre-Columbian days, according to ethnobotanical studies of the plant.

are adapted to radically different habitats. The sweet potato likes it best when the mercury is about 75°F; it suffers below 50°F, a temperature at which the potato thrives. True, both crops come from under the ground and both can be boiled, baked, and steamed. However, with respect to propagation, harvesting, and use, the differences are fundamental. The potato is an annual crop that dies off each year. Farmers hold over tubers to start the next crop. The sweet potato, by contrast, is a perennial. Its large roots store carbohydrates, and left alone, a stand of sweet potatoes can maintain itself for years. In the dry season, the foliage dies back and the unharvested roots survive underground. When rain returns, the old roots eventually resprout and send up new shoots. To start each crop cycle, farmers take stem cuttings or divide the tuberous roots and plant them in mounded hills. Sweet potato vines grow so fast and cover the ground so densely that the need for weeding is minimal. A family can harvest the vines; eat the tender, nutrient-rich foliage raw; and cook tougher leaves like spinach. The vines also make good forage for livestock.

The sweet potato's main turf today is in Asia, especially China, where 83 percent of the world's harvest is collected, about 107 million metric tons a year. Some

of this bounty is processed into starch for sweet potato noodles, dried and bleached into flour, or consumed fresh. Most of the nation's crop, however, is converted into nutritious hog feed—pork accounts for three quarters of China's meat production. By 2020, China's combined potato and sweet potato harvest is expected to reach 224 million metric tons, the dry-matter equivalent of 60 million metric tons of grain.

Cassava, *Manihot esculenta*, grows vegetatively from the plant's woody stalks. Cut down and saved at harvest, the stalks are stuck in the ground in sections at planting time, where they resprout and produce more tasty roots.

Follow in the steps of ancient Andean farmers and find out for yourself how easy it is to grow potatoes. Thanks to many centuries of cultivation, you can choose among hundreds of cultivars.

Manioc Matters

The Amazon's cassava, or manioc root (*Manihot esculenta*), is a mainstay today in tropical Asia, West Africa, and Brazil. Most commonly known in North America in the form of tapioca, cassava has even more fiber and carbohydrates than sweet potato. The crop is propagated vegetatively from the plant's woody stalks, which farmers cut down at harvest and store over the dry season. At planting time, they pile up soil in mounds and insert the stalks, which resprout when the rain comes. There are both sweet and bitter types of manioc: Both contain compounds that convert to cyanide, in amounts of greater or lesser toxicity. The sweet types can be cooked and eaten right after harvesting. The bitter types, however, must be soaked and rinsed to remove the toxins and then processed into starch—which is either made into a paste or dried into flour. How ancient peoples learned how to make edible a root that contains appreciable amounts of cyanide remains a mystery to this day.

The millennia-old relationship between people and food plants like potatoes, sweet potatoes, and manioc continues as new cultivars are developed with a view to improving their nutritional content and cultivation and as traditional, nearly forgotten uses of these ancient foodstuffs are revived and applied to the economies of the modern, ever hungry, world.

The International Potato Center

James J. Lang

On a small farm clinging to a Bolivian mountainside 15,000 feet above sea level, Carlos Huascar grows the traditional Andean tuber crops oca (*Oxalis tuberosa*), ulluco (*Ullucus tuberosus*), and mashua (*Tropaeolum tuberosum*), as well as 50 kinds of potatoes (*Solanum* species and hybrids), the radishlike maca root (*Lepidium meyenii*), dahlias, and artichokes. Huascar is part of the network of farmers working with the International Potato Center (better known as CIP, or Centro Internacional de la Papa) to preserve and promote the use of Andean crops largely unknown outside the region. Arracacha (*Arracacia xanthorrhiza*), ahipa (*Pachyrhizus ahipa*), mauka (*Mirabilis expansa*), yacón (*Smallanthus sonchifolius*), and achira (*Canna edulis*), which grow at lower altitudes in the milder, generally wetter lower valleys, are also part of the program. In addition, CIP created a cookbook and a television series in Ecuador called *Cocine con clase* (Cook With Class), which showcases Andean specialties and demonstrates how to prepare them.

These projects are just a small part of CIP's much larger agenda: to help farmers in poor countries around the world grow potatoes, sweet potatoes, and other crops more

sustainably. Throughout the developing world, CIP works with national programs and nongovernmental organizations and their agronomists and extension workers. The building blocks of CIP's work, though, are consultations with small-scale farmers and farmer training.

At its headquarters in Lima, Peru, CIP scientists have assembled the world's largest collection of potatoes, including more than 3,500 Andean cultivars from all eight

To preserve existing potato varieties, farmers working for the International Potato Center must replant the entire collection of over 3,500 cultivars each year.

In addition to potatoes, CIP promotes and preserves many other Andean tuber crops, such as oca, *Oxalis tuberosa*, which was first cultivated by the Incas.

domesticated potato species. The work required to maintain this collection is daunting. Unlike the seeds of a hard grain like rice, which can be put in cold storage for decades, potato tubers can only be kept from one growing season to the next. So CIP's network of farmers and agronomists replants, harvests, sorts, and stores its entire collection each year.

No domestic food crop has so large a clan of extant wild relatives as the potato, and CIP backs up its cultivated collection with a vast gene pool comprising 235 wild potato species. It is this treasure trove of genetic traits, both wild and cultivated, that CIP scientists draw on to fortify the potato against enemies such as late blight, the fungal disease that decimated Ireland's potato crop in the 1840s. CIP's network of breeders, extension agents, and farmers test varieties that show resistance to the disease in late-blight danger zones all over the world.

CIP's priorities also include pest management, disease-free seed multiplication, and tuber storage. For protection against pests like tuber moths and weevils, CIP teaches farmers defensive production practices; how to use pheromone traps and safe, biologically based insecticides; and how to entice potatoes' natural enemies. Because high potato yields depend to a great extent on the quality of the seed potatoes planted, CIP distributes cuttings taken from disease-free mother plants to farmers in the highlands of East Africa. In India, where storing potatoes is expensive, CIP promotes technologies to produce true botanical seed en masse. In the Andes, where farmers hold over seed tubers, CIP has pioneered the use of airy, diffusely lit aboveground storage as an alternative to traditional dark, dank, underground pits to keep seed potatoes firm and healthy.

Encyclopedia of Edible Tubers

Scott D. Appell

As you browse the following pages, you will encounter a wide array of tuberous plants that have sustained people in various parts of the world for centuries and even millennia. Originally cultivated for their nutritious underground storage organs, most of the plants featured on these pages can serve as lovely ornamental additions to the garden when integrated with annuals, herbaceous perennials, and shrubs. Where winters are cold, tropical and subtropical plants are stunning accents in a mixed summer border or container display, then transfer easily indoors when the days get cooler. In winter, feature them as showstopping houseplants or harvest a few tubers and cook up mouthwatering dishes. Hardy plants can stay in the ground year-round, providing an appealing floral display in spring or summer and hearty nourishment in fall and winter.

In addition to photographs of foliage, flowers, and tubers, each encyclopedia entry offers a brief introduction to the plant's place in human culinary history, a description of its ornamental features, details on how to grow and propagate it, and how to prepare the tasty tubers for eating. Always bear in mind that some tubers, like potatoes, for example, may be inedible or even poisonous in their raw state and must be cooked to make them palatable. Also see "Foraging for Wild Tubers," on beginning on page 98, for more information on identifying and gathering tubers in the wild.

To find out in which hardiness zone you garden, check the recently updated map of USDA hardiness zones at www.arborday.org/media/zones.cfm.

Oca, *Oxalis tuberosa*

Alocasia macrorrhiza

Giant Taro, Elephant's Ear, Ape (Hawaiian)

Giant taro originated in India and Sri Lanka. Over time its cultivation moved eastward across Oceania and the Pacific islands. Polynesian voyagers brought the plant to the Hawaiian Islands—whose residents call it ape (pronounced AH-pay)—about 1,500 years ago. Giant taro and other aroids (members of the plant family Araceae) are now a major food source in tropical areas around the world where it is too hot, humid, or wet for other carbohydrate-rich crops. Don't confuse giant taro with taro (*Colocasia esculenta*), a staple carbohydrate of the South Pacific, the Caribbean, and Antilles (see page 36).

Ornamental Attributes This warm-zone perennial can be massive, sometimes attaining 12 to 15 feet in height and 6 to 8 feet in width. Its dark green, arrowhead-shaped blades can grow to 4 feet in length. Giant taro will make a bold tropical statement in any indoor or outdoor landscape; it is quite exceptional in form.

Growing Tips The upright-growing tubers should be planted vertically, half in, half out of the soil; be sure to keep the root end down and the growing tip up. When in doubt, plant it horizontally—the plant will grow accordingly. Giant taro prefers a well-drained, humus- or compost-rich soil in semishade with high humidity. Keep it moist, watering freely in high temperatures, and feed it three times a month with an all-purpose, water-soluble organic fertilizer. Giant taro requires a long growth period—18 to 24 months between planting and harvesting is typical. Its tropical origin makes it quite suitable for gardens in the Deep South. In colder regions move it into a greenhouse or conservatory over the winter. Use an adequately-sized container and set the plant in an eastern, western, or southern exposure. Keep moist but not muddy, and don't the let the pot sit in a saucer of water—overwatering can be lethal. Beware of mealy bugs and spider mites indoors. Treat these with horticultural oil or an organic insecticide. You can withhold water to allow taro to become dormant and store the rhizome in a cool, frost-free area in its pot, or unpotted in damp, not wet, peat. The tubers can be harvested at any desired size in the South, where they can grow to weigh several pounds (one tuber can often feed an entire family). In the North, they are eaten when dug in autumn.

Propagation Propagate giant taro by removing offsets or dividing the rhizomes. Remove the offsets at any time in the South and in the spring before replanting in northern zones.

Hardiness USDA Zones 10 and 11

Cultivars and Related Species The 8-to 10-foot-tall *Alocasia* 'Variegata' has blades irregularly marked with ivory, gray-green, and white. 'Violacea' has purple-tinged foliage. The leaves of the variably patterned 'Lutea' are blotched yellow with a yellow mid-rib and stem.

Cooking and Eating Giant taro's lozenge-shaped, rough-skinned tubers are dark brown with a white interior and usually 8 to 10 inches long by 5 inches wide. (For a photo of the tuber, see page 10.) When cooked the tubers have a potato-like flavor—they make great "tropical home fries." The white interior of the thick stems can also be cooked, dried, and ground into an easily digested flour. Like most aroids, all parts of this edible species contain crystals of the chemical compound calcium oxalate, making it not only bitter and unpleasant tasting when uncooked but also the source of intense discomfort—as if thousands of needles were piercing the lips, mouth, and throat—when even the tiniest amount is chewed raw. Handle the plant and its parts carefully. The heat of cooking breaks down the crystals and renders the tubers edible.

Giant taro tubers are often simply boiled and eaten in curries and stews. Cook them like potatoes—until fork tender—10 to 20 minutes, depending on size. They are tasty mashed and cooked in coconut cream with dried shrimp.

Nutritional Value The giant taro is a good source of vitamin C, phosphorus, and iron and has a high energy value.

Amorphophallus konjac

Devil's Tongue, Konjac, Konnyaku (Japanese)

Devil's tongue, an eastern Asian native, is widely cultivated in southern China and Vietnam as a food crop and is an important carbohydrate source in Japan. While most people grow this plant for its corms, its foliage can also be cooked as a vegetable and in some regions is fed to pigs. In the Philippines, the young cooked shoots are considered a delicacy, much like asparagus.

Ornamental Attributes The plant gets its common name devil's tongue from its flowering part: a very tall (12 inches or more), stiff, mottled purple spike (spadix) that juts out of a purplish-red spathe. The bloom's foul smell attracts its pollinator, the carrion beetle. (In cooler regions, where it is grown as an annual, it rarely blooms.) The plant produces a large, solitary leaf divided into numerous leaflets, supported by an erect, 3-foot, puce-speckled leaf stalk. Its palmlike appearance lends a tropical air to the garden.

Growing Tips This plant is quite susceptible to wind damage and sunscald, so a sheltered site in 50 to 60 percent shade works best. Plant the corms at least 6 inches deep in well-drained, fertile soil. Devil's tongue benefits from liberal applications of manure or compost tea. Its growing period ranges from May through September, when the leaf begins to wither. The plant then becomes dormant and requires a distinct, four- to five-month dry period. In colder regions, grow it in a bulb pan or wide, shallow container, such as an azalea pot, outdoors in summer. Store it indoors during its dormancy at temperatures of 60° to 68°F.

Propagation Propagate devil's tongue from fresh seeds, which germinate in a matter of weeks, or by removing and potting up offsets from mature corms.

Hardiness USDA Zones 10 and 11

Cultivars and Related Species The tubers of another species, *Amorphophallus variabilis,* are cultivated and eaten in parts of Indonesia, where the plant is known as kembang bangké.

Cooking and Eating The black-skinned, spherical corms of devil's tongue are about 12 inches in diameter and can weigh up to 22 pounds. The starchy, bland-flavored corms are best harvested when small and sweet—when the plant is about a year old. They store quite well at 50°F. You can cook baby corms by washing and rubbing them with salt to expel excess moisture, followed by rinsing and dicing. Then either stir-fry them with other vegetables or simmer them in soy sauce. To make flour, the corms are washed, peeled, sliced or grated, and rinsed several times before being boiled in water. The starch that settles out is dried, sieved, and solidified with dissolved lime into an edible gray, tofu-like gel called konnyaku or yam cake. The noodles made from this cake, called shirataki, are used in the one-pot Japanese dish sukiyaki. In Korea, konnyaku is valued as a chewy addition to dishes like yachae chongol, a one-pot sukiyaki-like dish served over a burner at the table.

Nutritional Value Devil's tongue corms contain beta carotene, thiamin, and a number of minerals, including magnesium and manganese. The corms are rich in glucomannan, a calorie-free, soluble fiber that may have beneficial effects on cholesterol levels and on blood-sugar levels in diabetics.

Apios americana

Groundnut, Potato Bean, Indian Potato

The groundnut is native throughout a wide expanse of North America, from New Brunswick west to Colorado and south to Texas and Florida. Native Americans throughout this range valued this versatile plant. The edible roots can be found just beneath the surface of the soil, tightly clustered below the stem or in chains—sausage-link style—on long slender roots. The Cherokee used the roots like potatoes. The Delaware and Mohegan peoples dried the tubers and ground them into flour for bread and cakes. Wisconsin's Menominee tribe sugared the tubers with maple syrup. The Pawnee, Omaha, and Winnebago clans ate the tubers roasted or boiled. Many groups harvested, peeled, sliced, and dried the tubers for winter use. Native Americans shared their knowledge of this useful wild edible with early Europeans, helping the Pilgrims to survive their first winter in America. The groundnut may have been introduced into Europe as early as 1597 and was reportedly an important forage food during the Civil War. If you are tempted to go looking for groundnuts, check the U.S. Department of Agriculture's Natural Resources Conservation Service at http://plants.usda.gov/threat.html to find out if the plant is listed as threatened or endangered in your state. If it is safe to gather, see "Foraging for Wild Tubers," page 97, for tips on responsible wild collection.

Ornamental Attributes The groundnut is a perennial twining vine (unusual in that twines to the left), ranging from 3 to 10 feet in height. From July through September, it produces fragrant pink to mauve, or rarely maroon, sweet pea–shaped flowers. The long, slender seedpods are dehiscent—they expel their seeds forcefully when they reach maturity.

Growing Tips Groundnut prefers a moist environment and is frequently encountered in marshy areas or by streams or lakes in sunny spots. Hard frost will kill off the top growth. This legume is not fussy about soil quality—like many legumes it fixes its own nitrogen—as long as the soil is kept moist. It prefers a pH of 6.0 to 7.5 in full sun. Space plants 4 to 6 feet apart to provide good air circulation and avoid competition. Provide plant supports: plastic string or galvanized wire strung between posts, chain-link fencing, or erect tepee-style structures. You can harvest the tubers after one year (in late summer or fall), but two to three years of growth will produce the largest roots.

Propagation Propagate plants by seed or replant undersized tubers.

Hardiness USDA Zones 4 to 8

Cultivars and Related Species
Louisiana State University developed a breeding line of *Apios americana* (#784) that forms numerous reddish-brown tubers about 2 inches in diameter. 'Aquarius' has large tubers but is not as productive as other strains. 'Draco' produces relatively small but notably well-flavored and abundant tubers, 'Tyra' bears very large tubers with smooth skin.

Cooking and Eating Groundnut roots are generally pear-shaped and grow anywhere from an inch in diameter to as large as a chestnut, with a white and crisply textured interior. The rust- or red-skinned tubers have a sweet, starchy, faintly turniplike taste. You can eat the tubers raw, boiled, fried, roasted, or otherwise like potatoes. Add them to soups, stews, and casseroles; fry them; or mash and use in breads. Prepare the fresh or dried seeds as you would peas or beans.

Nutritional Value Groundnut contains up to 17 percent crude protein, more than three times that of potatoes.

Arisaema triphyllum

Jack-in-the-Pulpit, Indian Turnip

This beloved native wildflower of the deciduous forests of northeastern North America has a longstanding and important place among the pharmacopoeias of Native Americans. Its corms were the basis of pain relievers, antiflatulents, cough remedies, skin aids, and other medicines. Some native groups also ate them: The Potawatomi people of modern-day Wisconsin sliced the corms and cooked them in a pit oven for three days to break down the acridity. Menominee tribes in Illinois shredded the corms and boiled them with venison.

Ornamental Attributes Jack-in-the-pulpit is a spreading perennial that produces one or two leaves per corm, each divided into three narrow, oblong leaflets (hence the species name, *triphyllum*). The plants bear a distinctive hooded, green-and-purple-striped spathe in spring to early summer, followed by large, showy clusters of red berries in fall.

Growing Tips Jack-in-the-pulpit prefers moist but well-drained, neutral to acidic, humus-rich soil in a cool, partially shaded site. For harvesting, dig the corms in early spring (when the ground is just workable and long before any signs of aboveground growth). At that time, the corms are chock-full of carbohydrates in preparation for active growth and plump for eating. Likewise, the corms can be dug in late autumn when they are equally plump in preparation for hibernal dormancy.

Propagation Remove offsets from the corms and replant from the parent plant in fall. Offsets can be removed in late summer or through fall when the plants are dormant. Jack-in-the-pulpit can also be grown from seed, but be prepared to wait several seasons for full-size plants. Sow seed in containers in a cold frame in autumn or spring.

Hardiness USDA Zones 4 to 9

Cultivars and Related Species *Arisaema triphyllum* 'Black Jack' bears wonderful purple-black foliage and well-striped spathes. *A. tortuosum*, a native of Nepal, is considered quite succulent. The Lepchas of northern India use them to prepare a dish called tong. They bury the corms in masses until fermentation sets in, then dig them up, wash them, and cook them, alleviating their poisonous properties. This tall species (hardy in Zones 8 to 9) can attain 5 feet in height and produces hooded green spathes 4 to 7 inches long.

Cooking and Eating The small corms have tan to reddish-brown skin and creamy-white to light gray flesh. They have a bland, starchy flavor and taste best with a good sauce. As with all aroids, it is critical to carefully prepare jack-in-the-pulpit to break down the calcium oxalate crystals and make it edible. Traditional processing techniques include cutting the corms into very thin slices and allowing them to dry for several months, after which they can be eaten like potato chips, crumbled to make a cereal, or processed into a very fine flour. They can also be sliced and roasted and then ground to make a slightly cocoa-flavored product for use in pancakes and baked goods such as cakes, cookies, rolls, and muffins.

Nutritional Value The very fine starch is easily digestible.

Boesenbergia rotunda

Chinese Keys, Fingerroot, Krachai (Thai), Temu Kunci (Indonesian)

Chinese keys are thought to be indigenous to the Indonesian islands of Java and Sumatra and are cultivated from India and Sri Lanka to Thailand, Malaysia, Indonesia, and Vietnam (where it is known as bong nga truat). They have also become an important food and spice plant in central Asian countries, Russia, and even Hungary. Rhizomes and roots are used in soups and stews, made into pickles, and added to sambals (chile-based condiments). Their cooling, refreshing properties make Chinese keys a popular food in extreme heat, accompanying ice-cold rice. The roots are used medicinally in Southeast Asia and China. Scientists in Thailand have shown that the roots and rhizomes possess antibacterial properties, especially effective against intestinal microfauna.

Ornamental Attributes This member of the wildly versatile and widely distributed ginger family is a perennial herb to about 2½ feet tall with large, medium-green to bluish-green, elliptical, prominently veined leaves. It has an overall resemblance to the well-known but unrelated cast-iron plant (*Aspidistra elatior*) and adds a tropical air to shade-dappled container gardens and solariums. In August, pretty twin flowers, each with pale pink outer lobes and a darker rose-pink lip, are borne on erect stems close to the ground, well below the foliage.

Growing Tips *Boesenbergia rotunda* grows easily in tropical climates in humus-rich, water-retentive but well-drained soil in dappled shade. Avoid sites with burning sun and drying winds. In northern locales, cultivate Chinese keys in large containers (8 inches wide or larger) in an unobstructed east window or bay window, sunroom, or greenhouse. Indoors, watch for mealy bugs and spider mites. When growing the plant in containers, use a standard upright flowerpot to facilitate the unobstructed growth of the distinctive short, rounded (hence the species epithet) rhizome, which bears downward-growing, finger-like orange-brown-skinned roots. The fleshy underground structure is supposedly reminiscent of a set of Chinese keys, hence the common name; another common name, fingerroot, is more self-evident. Harvest the roots and rhizomes at any time of the year.

Propagation The short, branching rhizomes are easily divided vertically and can be replanted at any time of the year. Seed is rarely used for propagation

Hardiness USDA Zones 8 to 10

Cultivars and Related Species There are no other cultivated members of this genus.

Cooking and Eating The rhizomes and roots of Chinese keys are bright yellow on the inside and have an aromatic, spicy flavor. Fresh rhizomes and the hearts of the stems are eaten raw as a side dish with rice. The young leaves and shoots, along with fresh rhizomes, are finely chopped and mixed with grated coconut and spices, wrapped in a banana leaf, and steamed. In Thailand, the fresh rhizomes and roots are eaten raw in salads or with khao chae (a refreshing summertime rice dish); they are also added to fish curries, soups, pickles, and khanom chine (soft rice noodles with spicy curry). As a spice, small amounts are chopped or grated and added to curries, mixed vegetable soups, and other savory dishes. The roots and rhizomes will keep for a couple of months in a ventilated bag in the produce drawer of the refrigerator. For longer cold storage, they may be kept in large glass jars and covered with sherry or vodka, which becomes infused with the aromatics and may subsequently be incorporated into sauces or soups.

Nutritional Value There is little nutritional value in Chinese keys, but the fresh or dried rhizomes and roots are widely used as an aromatic digestive medicine to treat colic, flatulence, indigestion, diarrhea, and dysentery.

Canna edulis

Edible Canna, Queensland Arrowroot, Achira (Spanish)

Canna has spread from its probable site of origin in the Andes to cultivation in Mexico, the West Indies, and parts of South America. It has recently become an important industrial starch crop in northern Australia, hence its common name Queensland arrowroot. The rhizomes remain an important carbohydrate in Peru and southern Ecuador, where they are boiled or baked, often as part of a traditional feast featuring roasted guinea pig, yacón (p. 68), and quinoa beer. When baked (often as long as 12 hours), the roots become translucent, sweet, and mucilaginous. Residents of Cuzco in southern Peru traditionally eat canna, called achira, at the festival of Corpus Christi. The rhizomes also provide an arrowroot-like starch, which is made into cakes in Colombia. The young shoots are cooked as a green vegetable, and the large leaves are used to wrap tamales. Immature seeds are cooked in bocoles (fat tortillas). In Vietnam, where it is known as dong rieng, _Canna edulis_ is grown on a large scale to make the popular transparent Vietnamese noodles.

Ornamental Attributes This canna has broad elliptical or oblong, medium-green leaves on erect, stiff stems and bears attractive slender, single orange to red flowers—wildly attractive to hummingbirds—atop 6½ foot stems. Once pollinated, the blossoms are followed by warty seed capsules bearing hard, round black seeds.

Growing Tips Site edible canna in rich, moisture-retentive soil in full sun for best results. Plant the rhizomes 3 to 5 inches below the soil surface. Add plenty of compost or rotted manure if the soil needs amending. You can harvest the tubers eight months after planting. In colder areas, dig them up after the first frost kills the tops. Harvest the vigorous terminal ends of young rhizomes for eating. Large older rhizomes can be quite fibrous. Harvest at any time in the South; in the North, harvest when you are lifting the rhizomes in fall for overwintering. Overwinter them in a cool, frost-free area in damp peat moss or potting soil. The canna leaf roller (_Calpodes ethlius_), found in Texas northeast to New York and southward through Florida and the Caribbean, relies on canna foliage as its larval food. This caterpillar of the Brazilian skipper butterfly can be a serious pest in Florida. The safest control is to hand-pick the caterpillars.

Propagation At harvest, keep enough small, firm, and disease-free rhizomes for replanting the following spring.

Hardiness Zones 10 to 11

Cultivars and Related Species *Canna coccinea*, commonly called Indian shot, is the source of an edible starch also once used for fabric finishing.

Cooking and Eating The robust rhizomes may be several inches thick and up to 2 feet long, bearing distinct growth scales and white skin tinged with purple. The interior is white, crisp, and fairly juicy. In a casserole or stew, canna looks and tastes similar to potato. (See page 85 for a recipe using canna starch noodles.)

Nutritional Value The dried rhizomes contain 80 percent starch, 10 percent sugar, 1 to 3 percent protein, and are rich in potassium.

Claytonia virginica

Spring Beauty, Fairy Spud

This lovely springtime ephemeral is found in moist woodlands and thickets and on sunny streambanks in eastern North America. Native Americans such as the Iroquois and Algonquin boiled and roasted the tubers for food. In at least one state—Massachusetts—spring beauty is now listed as endangered, and wild collecting of it (and other native species) has become quite controversial as the populations of many plants are being steadily reduced by habitat loss and other threats. Before you collect spring beauty in the wild, check the U.S. Department of Agriculture's Natural Resources Conservation Service at http://plants.usda.gov/threat.html to find out if the spring beauty has been listed as threatened or endangered in your state. If it is safe to gather, see "Foraging for Wild Tubers," page 97, for tips on responsible wild collection.

Ornamental Attributes *Claytonia virginica* is an early-spring-blooming succulent perennial that grows about 12 inches tall by 8 inches wide. It has dark-green linear foliage that may be as long as 6 inches and produces flower stalks with up to 15 delicate pink-tinged white flowers. This plant makes a lovely addition to a rock garden, native plant collection, or wildflower garden.

Growing Tips Spring beauty prefers a humus-rich but sharply drained soil; if your beds are too sodden, work in plenty of sharp sand or turkey grit. Avoid sites that remain wet during the winter months. Collect corms for eating while the plants are in bloom (which can be challenging, given the sizable number it takes to serve one person and the fact that the charming flowers must be sacrificed). Keep the damage to a minimum by replanting the tiniest tubers and letting the beds rejuvenate for a couple of years between harvests. You can also plant multiple beds and rotate the harvests among them.

Propagation Propagate spring beauty by sowing seed in fall or replanting the small corms.

Hardiness USDA Zones 5 to 9

Cultivars and Related Species As yet there are no cultivars of *Claytonia virginica*.

Cooking and Eating Spring beauty tubers have a flavor reminiscent of cooked chestnuts. Eat the starchy tubers raw, boiled, fried, or mashed. Add them to salads, soups, stews, savory turnovers, and pies. They can also be cooked with peas like new potatoes. Eat the young stems and leaves raw in salads, or steam or sauté them and serve as greens. The pretty flowers make an attractive edible garnish.

Nutritional Value The tiny tubers are high in potassium and vitamin A and are a good source of calcium and vitamin C.

Colocasia esculenta

Elephant's Ear, Cocoyam, Taro (Spanish), Yu, Yu Tou (Chinese)

Elephant's ear is thought to be indigenous to India, and it has been cultivated in Southeast Asia for 10,000 years, grown in or near ancient rice terraces. The ancient Greeks and Romans brought it to the Middle East, Egypt, and Mediterranean regions. Spanish and Portuguese explorers later carried the plant to Africa and the New World, where it remains an important food source. In economic terms, this is the most important aroid globally. Hawaiians slice and fry them to make taro chips or pulverize and ferment them into a starchy paste called poi, the national dish. Haitians shred raw taro corms to make acras, savory fritters made with mixed vegetables or fish. Taro balls stuffed with meat are popular in China. Throughout Asia, India, and the Caribbean the leaf blades, petioles, and runners of the plant are cooked and used as vegetables or stew thickeners. In Japan, the spadices are baked with pork or fish as a delicacy.

Ornamental Attributes Elephant's ear leaves are shaped like hearts or arrowheads and may reach 3 feet long and 2 feet wide, and the plant may grow to 5 feet high and wide. It makes an exotic, tropical-looking addition to a cold-climate annual border or containerized specimen on a terrace.

Growing Tips Cultivated varieties of *Colocasia esculenta* fall into two main categories: the eddoe (or eddo) type (sometimes referred to as *Colocasia esculenta* var. *antiquorum* or *C. esculenta* var. *globulifera*), which has a relatively small main corm surrounded by somewhat large and numerous cormels, and the dasheen or taro type (*C. esculenta* var. *esculenta*), with a large corm up to 12 inches long and 6 inches in diameter. Taro relishes a rich, moist or wet, slightly acid soil amended with plenty of compost or well-rotted manure and full sun to partial shade. Plant the corms outside about 4 to 6 inches deep after all danger of frost has passed, or start indoors in a container or flat and then harden them off and transplant to the bed. In northern zones, dig up the corms after the first hard frost has killed the top growth and store them in a dry, frost-free location. To harvest in frost-free areas, simply dig them up and collect at will. In the North, harvest when you dig the whole plant for winter storage. For photos of the corm, see pages 5 and 92.

Propagation You can easily grow taro from divisions of tubers. Divide tubers at any time in the south and prior to replanting in spring in the north.

Hardiness USDA Zones 9 to 11

Cultivars and Related Species The Hawaiian cultivar *Colocasia esculenta* 'Ohe', which makes excellent poi, is adapted to drier soils. The Chinese selection 'Bun-Long' has a white interior and conspicuous purple flecks; it retains a crispy texture when baked or boiled. 'Mano Keokeo' corms are excellent baked or steamed.

Cooking and Eating This versatile vegetable's species name means succulently edible and reflects its potato-like flavor and moist texture. You can eat the corms—the carbohydrate-rich portion of the plant—boiled, fried, baked, steamed, baked au gratin, and incorporated into soups, stews, curries, and puddings, and dumplings. (See page 93 for an African recipe.) Commercially prepared starch, wrappers, doughs, and other taro products are available at specialty food stores.

Nutritional Value: Taro is a good source of vitamin C, phosphorus, and iron.

Dahlia Hybrids

Dahlia

Dahlias are native to the mountainous areas of Mexico south to Colombia. The pre-Columbian people of central Mexico, the Yucatán, and Guatemala valued the roots both for their nutritious inulin (a fructose sugar stored in the tubers of various plants of the daisy family) and for the antibiotic compounds concentrated in the tubers' skins. A sweet extraction of the roots called dacopa is used in beverages and flavorings, often mixed with water or milk or sprinkled on ice cream. Its naturally sweet, mellow taste is said to combine the flavors of coffee, tea, and chocolate.

Ornamental Attributes The beloved dahlia flower blooms from midsummer to first frost in a sizzling array of colors from vivid reds to pinks to shades of white, yellows darkening to orange and bronze, and purple hues from lilac to almost black, in various sizes, patterns, and forms. All told, there are an amazing 20,000 or so cultivars of the 30 dahlia species, and all are said to be edible. Dahlias are bushy, usually tuberous-rooted perennials with dark green leaves 8 to 20 inches long and divided into oval leaflets with toothed margins and rounded tips. The stiff, hollow stems support plants that may vary in height from less than 1 foot to a towering 15 feet tall.

Growing Tips Dahlias like humus-rich, well-drained soil in full sun and appreciate a weekly application of a high-nitrogen liquid fertilizer in early summer, then a high-potassium liquid fertilizer every week from midsummer to early autumn. It's best to choose a fertilizer that's approved for organic production. Gardeners in Zone 9 and points south can grow dahlias as perennials. Cut them back, mulch heavily, and leave in place. Further north, lift the tubers and move them indoors over the winter. Simply cut down the stems, dig up the clumps of tubers, brush off any excess soil, and leave the cluster to dry naturally upside down. When dried off, dust with an environmentally sound fungicide suitable for food crops and pack in boxes of vermiculite or dry sand and store over winter.

Propagation In spring divide the crown of tubers; leave a "neck" of the original stem on each tuber (the new shoots will emerge from this stem). Plant them outdoors after the soil has thoroughly warmed or start indoors in containers then transplant into the garden.

Hardiness USDA Zones 9 to 11

Cultivars and Related Species Of the innumerable options out there, *Dahlia imperialis*, the imperial or tree dahlia, makes an astonishing addition to the summer border. It can grow 15 feet or more, bears single mauve flowers, and is used as a food in its native Central America.

Cooking and Eating Dahlias have elongated tubers with gray-brown, slightly wrinkled skin and a white, crisp interior. For eating, choose tubers that are firm and not too large and woody. They can be boiled, roasted, or baked. See the recipe for dahlia tuber bread on page 88. Add the flowers to salads; the flavor seems to differ from color to color.

Nutritional Value The inulin content makes dahlia a safe food for diabetics.

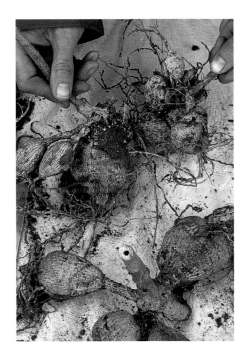

Dioscorea alata

White Yam, Air Potato, Ñame (Spanish)

The English common name for this group of plants, yam, is based on the Spanish word ñame and the Portuguese inhame, which are both based on the Wolof (the language of Senegal, Gambia, and Mauritania) verb nyami, "to eat"— a testament to the importance of this plant to many Africans. This species, the white yam, originated in eastern Asia and is now widely grown in India, Malaysia, Thailand, and China. About a thousand years ago travelers took it to East Africa and later, about 1500, to the West Indies with the slave trade. The tubers themselves develop singly or sometimes in a bunch, penetrating the soil as deeply as 7 feet. In the torpor-producing humidity of the tropics, harvesting them is a laborious process indeed, considering that they can attain the astonishing length of 7 feet and tip the scales at 150 pounds!

Ornamental Attributes This twining climber has glossy, heart-shaped, distinctly veined leaves and may reach a height of 12 feet. It bears small edible tubers called bulbils in the leaf axils.

Growing Tips Plant seed tubers (similar to those of commercially produced potatoes and available from nursery catalogs) in full sun several inches deep in loose, fertile, well-drained soil amended with plenty of well-rotted manure or compost. Yam prefers the heat and humidity of the southern U.S., where it excels. Yam is considered invasive in parts of Florida, Louisiana, and Georgia. (Check with your cooperative extension service or invasive pest plant council before planting in these areas. Or visit the BBG website for information and a list of useful links at bbg.org/gar2/pestalerts/#invasive). In the North, use the plant as an annual where summers are typically long and hot (usually up to Zone 6). You can let the plants trail along the ground, but 12-foot-tall, tepee-style supports ease cultivation and harvesting, and facilitate good air circulation. (You can fashion supports by inserting posts into the ground and tying them together at the top like a tepee frame. Then run wire around the posts.) The vines are the larval food source for the Asian moth *Palpifer sordida*. Tubers are ready for harvesting eight to nine months after planting, when the vines begin to wither. Use great care when collecting the tubers to avoid injuring their skin and inviting rot. You can keep the tubers without refrigeration for up to six months.

Propagation When harvesting the large terrestrial tubers for consumption, you can slice off the top of the tuber

from where the shoots arise and replant these tops to make whole new, asexually propagated plants. Keep these just moist until the shoots develop, then harden them off and plant outside. Alternatively, you can plant the aerial bulbils whole.

Hardiness USDA Zones 10 and 11

Cultivars and Related Species Three Puerto Rican selections are worth experimenting with: *Dioscorea alata* 'Florido' produces high quality, compact tubers; it is also early sprouting and maturing and high yielding. 'Forastero' bears somewhat irregularly shaped but smooth-skinned tubers with superior cooking qualities. 'Gemelos' produces high yields of perfectly shaped cylindrical tubers.

Cooking and Eating The skin of yam varies from dark brown to light pink; it is difficult to peel but loosens when heated. The flesh varies from white to deep orange. The tubers contain an alkaloid known as dioscorine and must be cooked to be edible. They can be eaten boiled, roasted, and baked (see page 93 for a traditional British recipe for yam pudding). They can also be mashed, fried, made into chips, french fries, flours, or fufu (an African and Caribbean dish of boiled and pounded tubers similar to soft polenta). The small aerial tubers are consumed the same way.

Nutritional Value Yams are a good source of the antioxidant beta-carotene as well as vitamin C, magnesium, potassium, thiamin, and some iron.

Eleocharis dulcis

Chinese Water Chestnut, Ma Tai (Cantonese)

Chinese water chestnut, a native of the Far East, was introduced to the West in the 17th century. It is currently grown commercially in China, Japan, Taiwan, and Thailand, where it is cultivated paddy-style, in flooded fields that are drained before harvesting. Chinese water chestnuts are widely used in Chinese cuisine, especially "Western-style" dishes like chop suey. Flour or starch made from the pulverized dried tubers is used to thicken sauces and to give a crispy coating to deep-fried foods. In Zimbabwe, the plant is used as a salt substitute. The corms are burned, and the ashes are used as a seasoning.

Ornamental Attributes Water chestnut is a bog plant that grows in the shallows along the edges of deeper bodies of water. It has a tuft of slender, tubular leaves about 1½ to 3 feet tall arising from the rounded corm, which grows below the ground underwater. The linear architectural form of this plant makes it an interesting addition to a water garden.

Growing Tips Grow water chestnut in a large, flat, watertight container such as a sun-resistant wading pool, a prefabricated polymer water garden sunken into the soil and set up as a bog environment, an old bath tub, a salvaged water tank, or a clean oil drum cut in half. Plant the corms 2 inches deep in muck soils (heavy inundated soils), clay loam, or sandy loam in full sun. Keep the soil moist but not wet until the shoots are about 4 inches tall, then flood the container to a depth of 3 or 4 inches. After six or seven months, drain off the water and let the soil remain moist but not wet until the foliage withers. After about a month the corms are ready for harvesting. At the ends of slender underground runners you will find small seed corms as well as larger, storage corms good for eating. A single corm can produce 100 new corms by the end of the season, about 80 percent of which are large enough to eat. The rest can be stored for propagation in moist sand in a cool place. To get started you can buy fresh corms at a Chinese market.

Propagation Save seed corms in fall and plant them in spring.

Hardiness USDA Zones 10 and 11

Cultivars and Related Species As yet, there are no cultivars, although some less sweet forms are grown agriculturally and used as hog feed.

Cooking and Eating The rounded, turnip-shaped corms of water chestnuts are about 1½ inches in diameter and have an inedible and difficult-to-peel brown skin enclosing sweet-tasting bright white flesh. Unlike most vegetables, Chinese water chestnuts remain crisp even after they are cooked or canned because their cell walls are cross-linked and strengthened by phenolic compounds, a property shared by the tiger nut (*Cyperus esculentus*), sacred lotus (*Nelumbo nucifera*), and a few other vegetables. You can eat the sweet, crisp corms raw, cooked, or dried. They are often stir-fried in meat and vegetable dishes and used in fillings for sweet pastries or turnovers. (See page 87 for a recipe.)

Nutritional Value The corms contain a fair amount of minerals and vitamins, especially vitamin B6. They have a relatively low energy value, with 5 percent each of starch and sugars.

Ensete ventricosum

Enset, Abyssinian Banana, Ethiopian Banana

Ethiopia's Sidama and Gurage farmers have a saying: "Enset is our food, our clothes, our beds, our houses, our cattle-feed, our plates." To people in the densely populated south of Ethiopia, enset is the most important root crop; it has probably been cultivated in that region for at least 5,000 years. By some accounts enset produces more food per acre than most cereals. Among other uses, Ethiopians chop and grate the pulp of the corms and tender leaf sheaths, ferment the mixture for up to 20 days, then use the results as flour to make kocho, a flatbread traditionally served with kitfo (spiced, minced beef). Bulla, a more refined, starch-rich, flourlike product, is used to make various foods such as porridge, pancakes, and dumplings.

Ornamental Attributes In recent years enset has become a popular landscaping plant thanks to its huge, decorative leaves and tropical appeal. Enset is a single-stemmed perennial herb that can grow up to 30 feet tall. Its palmlike trunk has the same structure as its cousin, the banana (*Musa* species)—sheathing leaf bases. When the plants are mature they produce a single flower head that forms multiple fruits, flowers, and seeds. The entire head, which may be 3 feet in length, hangs down from a stalk emanating from the center of the foliage. This fruiting body is banana-like, but its fruits are dry and unpalatable. The pea-sized seeds are black and irregularly shaped.

Growing Tips Grow enset in the ground or in a large container that's at least 16 inches in diameter. Plant it in humus-rich soil in full sun. While the plant is grow-ing, water freely and apply a liquid, balanced organic fertilizer monthly. After two to three years of uninterrupted growth, enset will produce a corm that is large enough to harvest for eating. If you want to go that route, dig up the plant before it forms a flower head; cut back its aboveground stems, scrape the corm clean, and the white flesh is ready to be processed. Unless you are lucky enough to live in Zone 11, you will have to move enset inside in autumn and keep it in a greenhouse or sunroom. You can also dig up the corm, clean away the dead leaf sheaths, and store it in damp sand until spring and then replant.

Propagation Propagate enset via seed: Soak the seeds 24 hours in warm water before planting in individual pots; keep the pots warm and just moist. Germination takes place within three months. If you grow it under glass or indoors, be

on the lookout for spider mites and aphids. In frost-free zones termites can be a problem.

Hardiness USDA Zone 11

Cultivars and Related Species In its native Ethiopia there may be as many as 50 recognized selections. Of the cultivars available in North America, *Ensete ventricosum* 'Maurelii' has banana-like leaves tinged with red, especially along the margins, and dark red leaf stalks.

Cooking and Eating Enset's massive, rounded underground corm grows up to 3 feet in diameter. The flesh has a bland flavor reminiscent of cooked plantains. Amicho is an Ethiopian dish in which the young corms are prepared like potatoes, and this may be the easiest cooking method for the adventurous home gardener in North America. Other Ethiopian dishes, such as kocho, are much more labor intensive.

Nutritional Value The Ethiopian banana is rich in starch, protein, sugar, and minerals; it is also a good source of calcium.

Helianthus tuberosus

Jerusalem Artichoke, Sunchoke

Jerusalem artichokes are cultivated for their fleshy tubers, which resemble knobby, white-skinned potatoes and have crisp, white flesh. Jerusalem artichoke is native to North America, from Ontario and Saskatchewan south to Georgia, Tennessee, and Arkansas. It grows in damp places in good soil, and is often encountered in abandoned farmsteads and at the edges of woodlands. The name Jerusalem is often assumed to be a corruption of girasole, the Italian word for sunflower, and these plants do belong to the same genus as the garden sunflower, *Helianthus annuus*. This plant was an important food source for such Native American tribes as the Cherokee (of modern-day North Carolina), Micmac (Nova Scotia), Iroquois (upstate New York), and Potawatomi (Wisconsin), who ate them raw, boiled, or roasted. Native Americans foraged for the tubers for millennia, and some eventually began growing their own. In 1605 French explorer Samuel de Champlain found Indians on Cape Cod cultivating Jerusalem artichokes. The tubers of these cultivated forms were larger and less knobby than their wild counterparts.

Ornamental Attributes This perennial may grow up to 10 feet tall. Its erect stems and foot-long, lance-shaped foliage are coarsely hairy. In late summer to autumn, the plants bear 4-inch-wide, deep yellow flowers, typical of the sunflower family. Jerusalem artichoke is a valuable late-season bloomer for the perennial bed or border, and makes a great cut flower. Grown en masse, they can form an effective screen.

Growing Tips Jerusalem artichoke couldn't be easier to cultivate. Plants require only a moist, fertile, friable soil in a sunny location. Plant the tubers 3 to 4 inches deep and about 2 feet apart. The tubers are ready for harvesting when the first hard frost has killed back the tops, or about a month after flowering. Harvest regularly, as the plants can become an aggressive nuisance in an untended garden.

Propagation Plants are easily propagated using pieces of tuber. Before planting, rub the cut surfaces with a newly purchased cinnamon stick, an effective natural fungicide.

Hardiness USDA Zones 4 to 9

Cultivars and Related Species Not surprisingly, there is an extensive selection of Jerusalem artichoke cultivars. *Helianthus tuberosus* 'Brazilian' can occasionally reach 12 feet in height and produces abundant large, white-skinned tubers. An old French cultivar, 'Tuseau', produces large tubers like sweet potatoes, 4 to 5 inches long, with knob-free, tan skin. It grows 7 to 9 feet tall. Native Americans in northern Ontario developed 'Stampede', a high-yielding strain that bears large, white-skinned tubers, often as heavy as a half-pound apiece.

Cooking and Eating Eat the tubers peeled and raw in salads; in side dishes steamed, fried, baked, pickled, boiled or puréed; or treated like potatoes in soups, casseroles, and savory pies. (See page 88 for a Native American recipe for braised Jeruselem artichokes.) The tubers can be roasted and ground for a caffeine-free coffee substitute. Unlike most tubers, they store the carbohydrate inulin instead of starch, making this a safe food for diabetics—the human body cannot break down inulin. For this reason, Jerusalem artichoke tubers are an important source of fructose for the food industry. They are also used commercially in the production of gluten-free "artichoke pasta."

Nutritional Value Jerusalem artichoke is a good source of iron, potassium, and phosphorus.

Ipomoea batatas

Sweet Potato, Batata (Spanish)

Sweet potatoes are native to the northwestern area of South America, where they have been eaten for at least 10,000 years. Scientific investigations have indicated that Pre-Columbian voyagers brought sweet potatoes to Polynesia, and centuries later, Portuguese and Spanish explorers carried it from its native habitat to Europe, Africa, and Asia. In the West Indies and Africa, the starchier, white type is preferred, while the moist, orange-fleshed type is popular in most other parts of the world. These sweeter cultivars are often referred to as yams in the United States, not to be confused with the true yam (*Dioscorea alata*).

Ornamental Attributes This perennial trailing vine bears attractive heart-shaped leaves; older plants produce funnel-shaped purple, pink, or white flowers. In regions where it is not hardy, use this plant as an ornamental annual groundcover or as an underplanting for corn, sorghum, sunflowers, pole beans, and chayote squash.

Growing Tips Sweet potato requires subtropical heat to excel. Sweet potatoes prefer a sandy loam of average fertility and full sun. Avoid high-nitrogen fertilizers because plants will put forth too much foliar growth at the expense of tuber formation. Set plants 12 to 18 inches apart with 3 to 4 feet between rows. Depending on the cultivar, the roots are ready for harvest 60 to 90 days after planting. Harvest using a spading fork, taking care not to damage the tubers' skin. To deter rot, allow the tubers to dry on the ground two to three hours after digging, then place them in a warm room (85°F with 85 percent humidity). After 10 to 14 days store them in a cool (55°F) location. For a photo of the tuber, see page 15.

Propagation Plants are typically propagated through stem cuttings (semiripe tip cuttings using rooting hormone) or divisions of the tubers. When harvesting the root for consumption, you can slice off the top and replant it to make new asexually propagated plants. Keep these just moist until the shoots develop, then harden them off and plant outside.

Hardiness USDA Zones 10 and 11

Cultivars and Related Species There are two types of sweet potato cultivars. Most "dry flesh" cultivars have yellow or white flesh and are mealier and less sweet than "moist flesh" types. *Ipomoea batatas* 'Ivoire' has white skin and flesh and is dry, dense, and starchy. 'Mexican Purple' bears very large tubers, up to 5 pounds each, with brownish-red skin and flesh that turns deep purple when cooked; it

has a nutlike flavor. Moist-flesh cultivars (the forms with dark yellow or orange-red interiors mistakenly called "yams") include 'Vardaman', which has golden-yellow and deep orange flesh and is considered superior for eating. 'Garnet' has large, fairly uniform tubers with handsome, reddish-purple skin and dark orange, very moist, flavorful flesh. It is excellent for baking.

Cooking and Eating This plant, a cousin of the garden morning glory (*Ipomoea tricolor*), has a tuberous root that is oblong or almost spherical in shape, with a smooth skin that ranges from red, purple, and brown to white. Its flesh can be white, yellow, orange, or purple. You can eat the tubers raw (they're delicious simply sprinkled with

sea salt), boiled and mashed, steamed, baked, fried, or batter-fried as tempura. The flesh is cooked in pies, cakes, breads, puddings, custards, cookies, ice cream, candies, jams, dulce de batata, and other desserts. It can also be dried for later use. Boiled sweet potato leaves are a common side dish in Taiwanese cuisine, often boiled with garlic and vegetable oil and sprinkled with salt before serving. See page 92 for an Indonesian recipe.

Nutritional Value Sweet potatoes are exceptionally nutritious. They contain high-quality protein and substantial quantities of vitamins A, B6, and C. Selections with dark orange flesh are richer in vitamin A.

Lathyrus tuberosus

Earth Chestnut, Tuberous Vetch

This little wildflower is found in hedgerows, vineyards, fields, and meadows throughout much of Europe and beyond, from France and Spain eastward across Russia to Siberia and southward to Turkey and western Iran. It is not found in Ireland or Portugal. It has been introduced into Great Britain, Denmark, and Sweden, where it flourishes. The amylaceous (having or resembling starch) tubers were collected and eaten by the Kalmyk people, who have lived in the Lower Volga region for nearly 400 years. In 1783, it was introduced into France from Holland, where it was cultivated and the tubers brought to market. The small, dark-skinned tubers are sometimes called Dutch mice.

Ornamental Attributes This delicate, tendriled vine clambers to about 3 feet tall. The 2-inch leaves are oval with a fine point. The typically pea-shaped flowers are fragrant, mauve-pink to crimson, up to an inch long, and are borne on slender stems from June through August. Earth chestnut has a long flowering period and is suitable for a meadow garden. It makes an excellent if somewhat lax cut flower. Pick it in the morning to prolong its vase life. The flowers are followed by small, brown, pealike pods containing 3 to 6 seeds.

Growing Tips This nitrogen-fixing plant is not fussy about soil fertility as long as it is not acidic or soggy. It does need full sun and requires supports, such as inverted branches, hand-hewn tepees of bamboo or willow, or rustic trellises. The vine can also serve as erosion control on a rough bank; cultivate it without any support and it will happily sprawl over the ground. Earth chestnut is considered a good bee plant. Unfortunately, slugs are also inordinately fond of this crop and can decimate an entire planting if not diligently removed.

Propagation To propagate earth chestnut by seed, presoak autumn-collected seed in early spring for 24 hours in warm water, sow in communal pots, and germinate in a cold frame or sow seeds outdoors in midspring. You can also divide the tubers when the plants are dormant in early spring or autumn. This plant is low yielding and is better considered a tasty treat rather than a staple crop.

Hardiness USDA Zones 6 to 11

Cultivars and Related Species At this time, no breeding or selection programs have been carried out with *Lathyrus tuberosus,* but the earth chestnut would be an excellent candidate especially when selected for tuber size and quantity. *Lathyrus odoratus,* the sweet-scented decorative annual sweetpea, is a close relative.

Cooking and Eating The black-skinned tubers are 1 to 3 inches in diameter and are borne by thin underground rhizomes. They taste bland and chewy when eaten raw but develop an agreeable flavor that is somewhat reminiscent of sweet potato or chestnut when they are boiled or roasted. In Scotland the tubers are used to flavor whiskey.

Nutritional Value These tubers, though rather tasty, are low in nutrients.

Manihot esculenta

Cassava, Manioc, Tapioca Plant, Yuca (Spanish)

Cassava tubers have smooth, reddish-brown skin and mealy chalk-white or yellowish flesh. Modern cassavas are the result of the hybridization and selection of several wild species by the Amerindians of the Amazon Delta, where the plant originated. (The earliest archaeological records, from coastal Peru, date to about 1000 B.C.) Most—but not all—modern commercial cultivars are "sweet" varieties, which have been developed over the centuries and can be eaten raw. They have a potato-like flavor but are firmer than potatoes; when raw they're woody and become much softer when cooked. By contrast, some primitive varieties are bitter tasting and contain potentially toxic concentrations of cyanogenic glycosides. In traditional communities of the Americas, people laboriously processed the tubers to make them edible by peeling, grating, washing, squeezing, drying, and then cooking and sometimes fermenting them. (Imagine the hazardous culinary experimentation that occurred over the millennia!)

Ornamental Attributes This erect, shrubby plant grows up to 12 feet high and has large, ornate, deeply cut leaves. Cassava makes a great hedgelike backdrop for the potager. The variegated cultivar is particularly ornamental.

Growing Tips Cassava needs full sun and regular moisture for successful cultivation. The soil should be of average fertility but well drained. The plant tolerates a wide range of soil pH (from 4 to 8). Cassava plants need two to three years to develop a sizeable root. In cooler regions, cultivate cassava in a large tub or pot, summering it outdoors and bringing it in over the winter in a greenhouse or bay window. Watch for spider mites and mealy bugs indoors. Treat these with horticultural oil.

Propagation Propagate cassava by dividing the root or by taking cuttings. This plant qualifies as a "quick stick"—simply jab foot-long sections of stem (containing at least one node) 6 inches or so into the soil, and they will take root!

Hardiness USDA Zones 10 and 11

Cultivars and Related Species The ornamental selection Manihot esculenta 'Variegata' bears spectacular leaves with creamy-yellow centers and carmine-red leaf stalks. It is readily available from nurseries.

Cooking and Eating Tubers can grow quite large—up to 3½ feet long. Always assume the root must at least be cooked to be safely edible. Cassava can be boiled,

fried, or baked, or made into meal, sweet-meats, bammies (Jamaican flatbread) and other breads, farina, and fufu. The refined starch of the tubers (known as tapioca) is used in soups, puddings, and dumplings. In Cuban cuisine, boiled yuca con mojo (with olive oil, onions, garlic, cumin, and sour orange or lime juice) is very popular. Like an Irish potato, these tubers oxidize (darken) quickly when exposed to the air, so keep the skinned roots under water until you are ready to cook them. The tuber's flavor spoils in a day or so even if it's unskinned and refrigerated; supermarkets often solve this problem by sealing them in wax—hence the shiny appearance of grocery-store cassava. The tender young leaves are also used as a potherb.

Nutritional Value Cassava tubers contain significant amounts of calcium, phosphorus, and vitamin C but are poor in protein and other nutrients.

Maranta arundinacea

Arrowroot, Maranta (Spanish)

Archaeological studies in the Americas show evidence of arrowroot cultivation as early as 7,000 years ago. This plant's English name may be derived from the native Caribbean Arawak people's term aru-aru, meaning "meal of meals" because the tubers were a staple food for this group. It has also been suggested that the common name comes from the plant's use in treating poison-arrow wounds—the Arawaks were a warlike people. Arrowroot is also the name sometimes used to refer to *Canna edulis* rhizomes (see page 32), so bear this in mind when shopping for it in markets or at nurseries.

Ornamental Attributes In consistently warm regions, where it is a perennial, arrowroot may reach a height of 6 feet. From summer to winter, it bears paired, creamy-white flowers at the ends of delicate, slender branches. Although *Maranta arundinacea* is not grown as an ornamental as commonly as other *Maranta* species, it forms small clumps of attractive smooth, oval leaves from 2 to 10 inches in length and is available in a variegated form.

Growing Tips Outdoors, grow it in full sun to partial shade in humus-rich, moist but well-drained soil. In northern climates, cultivate it as a container plant in a rich soilless or soil-based mixture. Fertilize monthly with an organic fertilizer when in active growth. Its humidity requirements (as high as 90 percent) lends it to conservatory culture. Watch out for mealy bugs and spider mites indoors. You can also let it go dormant and keep it warm and moist but not overly wet. Arrowroot needs 10 or 11 months of warm, moist weather to form mature tubers.

Propagation Divide the clumps anytime during active growth or when the plant is completely dormant. The tubers should be planted about 6 inches deep and spaced about 15 inches apart.

Hardiness Warmer regions of USDA Zones 9 to 11

Cultivars and Related Species The variegated form *Maranta arundinacea* 'Variegata' (pictured at left) features pale cream-colored splotches on the leaves, which brightens up the foliage. The related West Indian plant *Calathea allouia*, known as sweet corn root in English and lerén in Spanish,

has an agreeable flavor similar to sweet corn; it is considered a gourmet item in Puerto Rico and the Lesser Antilles (see recipe on page 90). The delicious small white tubers can be simply boiled and eaten as a side dish or sauced as an entrée; it is a traditional Christmas dish in the Dominican Republic. The care and culture is the same as for arrowroot.

Cooking and Eating This tropical perennial produces numerous fleshy, pendulous tubers, tapered at both ends and covered with large, thin scales that leave prominent rings of scars. The tubers are delicious—lightly sweet and crisp. They are eaten raw, roasted, grated into a coarse meal, or made into arrowroot powder. The highly digestible starch is used for pastries and biscuits and to thicken soups, sauces, and gravies. West Indian arrowroot, the finest of which comes from the Bermudas, is made from the year-old roots. The tubers are beaten to a pulp in large, deep vessels, then mixed with water. The fibrous parts are separated out, and the milky liquid is strained through a sieve. The starch is allowed to settle, the clear fluid is poured off, and the starch is then dried on sheets in the sun.

Nutritional Value The boiled tubers are a good source of calcium and are considered a beneficial, easily assimilated food for infants, the elderly, and people who are ill or who have trouble digesting other starches.

Nelumbo nucifera

Sacred Lotus, Lian (Chinese)

Sacred lotus's native habitat spans a huge geographic area from Afghanistan to Vietnam, and from there it has been distributed widely as an ornamental and food plant. The Chinese have cultivated lotus for at least 14,000 years, and it remains an important food there as well as a sacred symbol of eternal life. It is also the national flower of India. The species name *nucifera* means "nut-bearing," a reference to the plant's edible seeds, which are eaten raw, roasted, boiled, pickled, or candied.

Ornamental Attributes Young lotus leaves float on the water surface, and as the season progresses, new leaves reaching 2½ feet in diameter grow as much as 5 feet above the water on strong, erect stalks. The fragrant, solitary flowers, which range in color from snow white to yellow to light pink, may be a foot wide and are produced on rigid stems rising several feet above the water. The plant normally grows upward and has a horizontal spread of up to 9 feet.

Growing Tips Lotus rhizomes are 6 to 10 inches long and grow in chains like sausage links on or just below the surface of pond or river bottoms. Their many air-filled channels make them very buoyant; to get them to root properly, they must be held down with rocks or other weights when planting. In an outdoor pond, pool, or large waterproof container, grow sacred lotus in heavy loam enriched with well-rotted manure or soil mix, in full sun. It requires several weeks above 80°F to bloom. Fertilize twice monthly during active growth with tablet-form aquatic plant fertilizer. In northern regions, cultivate it as a greenhouse aquatic in a half-barrel container.

Propagation Grow sacred lotus from rhizomes, available at Asian markets, or from seeds. The pale tan seeds sold in Asian grocery stores are already shelled and won't germinate, but seeds pried from pods used in flower arrangements will germinate quite quickly after being rubbed with a file to wear down the hard seed coat.

Hardiness USDA Zones 4 to 11

Cultivars and Related Species Innumerable ornamental cultivars are available, but the Chinese have developed two cultivars specifically for the table: *Lotus nucifera* 'Man ha' is usually served cooked, and the early-blooming 'Zao Hua' is preferred raw. Native Americans collected and ate the tubers of North America's native species *Nelumbo lutea*. It grows to 6 feet tall and is also hardy in Zones 4 to 11.

Cooking and Eating Almost the entire plant is edible. The rhizomes are crisp and moist, like water chestnut, with an almondlike flavor. Slice through the light tan flesh of a rhizome to reveal the pretty pattern of oval or circular air channels within. You can eat them raw, boiled, pickled, stir-fried, deep-fried as tempura, or preserved in sugar. (For a salad recipe, see page 90.) The seeds are equally versatile. Eat the young foliage raw, tossed with sesame oil in salads, and use the older leaves as wrappers for steamed dim sum. The flowers make an edible garnish.

Nutritional Value The rhizomes contain 6 percent starch and 2 percent protein and are rich in minerals and vitamins. The nuts are very nutritious, with 60 percent starch, 15 percent protein, and only 2 percent fat.

Oxalis tuberosa

New Zealand Yam, Oca (Spanish)

Oca is an ancient Incan crop, indigenous to the Andean highlands in South America, where it is second only to the potato in importance. Oca is still cultivated from Venezuela to northern Argentina at altitudes of 9,000 to 12,000 feet. It has recently become a fairly significant crop in Mexico, where it is known as papa roja, or "red potato." Although it is rarely encountered outside specialty markets in the U.S., it was introduced in New Zealand around 1860 and has since gained culinary popularity—and its common name in English, New Zealand yam.

Ornamental Attributes This herbaceous plant has an upright, bushy habit and grows to about 17 inches tall and 2 feet wide. Like many other species of *Oxalis*, Oca's leaves are typically composed of three leaflets, reminiscent of a shamrock. The thick stems are purplish and succulent. Oca would certainly make an out-of-the-ordinary border for the potager or herb garden.

Growing Tips Oca is easy to grow and care for. It excels in average soil and full sun and tolerates a wide pH range—5.3 to 7.8. Plant the tubers in spring immediately after the last frost date. You can easily propagate them from cuttings or tubers too small to eat. Oca is a short-day plant and does not begin to form tubers until the days are markedly shorter, in September. Harvest the tubers when the tops are killed by hard frost. Leave the freshly dug tubers in the sun (or on a sunny windowsill) for a week or so to break down their acidity and increase

sweetness. They keep wonderfully well for months in the vegetable drawer of the refrigerator, as long as you keep them dry. North of Zone 8, dig up the tubers and store them in barely damp sand for replanting in the spring, or cultivate them in a cool alpine house. Temperatures below 10°F will kill the tubers.

Hardiness USDA Zones 8 to 11

Cultivars and Related Species *Oxalis tuberosa* 'Mexican' has attractive velvety-looking wine-colored foliage and produces very crisp, juicy, mild-flavored tubers. 'Orange' produces cylindrical, wrinkled but glossy, orange- to yellowish-orange-skinned tubers with firm white flesh. 'Yellow' bears cylindrical, very wrinkled tubers with glossy yellow skin and firm white flesh.

Cooking and Eating Oca is often called "the potato that doesn't need sour cream" because the tubers' oxalic acid content makes them tart in taste. They are crisp,

slightly juicy, and wonderful to eat, with a flavor that's similar to garden sorrel, which also contains oxalic acid. The tubers range from 2½ to 4 inches in length and resemble small, stubby, wrinkled carrots or new potatoes. They can be white, yellow, pink, red, purple, or black, depending on the cultivar. Oca tubers are traditionally sun dried for a few days after harvesting to increase their sweetness (the glucose level may nearly double) and then boiled, roasted, or prepared as pachamanca (tubers, maize, and meat roasted underground using hot stones covered by grass and earth).

Nutritional Value The tubers contain up to 9 percent protein and are an excellent source of calcium and iron.

Pachyrhizus erosus

Yam Bean, Jícama (Spanish)

Jícama is a bean species cultivated not for its seeds or pods but for its large, crisp, juicy roots. This versatile plant evolved in Mexico and Central America and has been cultivated there since ancient times. In the 16th century, the Spaniards carried it to the Philippines, and from there it spread into Indonesia, the Far East, Mauritius, Réunion, and West Africa. It is now grown around the world but is especially favored in Southeast Asia and China.

Ornamental Attributes This twining, annual vine can easily grow 10 to 20 feet high in one long growing season and would make a good cover for unsightly outbuildings and fences or to block out unattractive neighboring properties or vistas. It has coarse, three-leafed foliage typical of the bean family. Since it is a short-day plant, in North American gardens it generally does not produce its lavender or white blossoms or fuzzy, 3½-inch-long seedpods until after the middle of September.

Growing Tips Jícama does best in a warm climate with moderate rainfall; it is quite sensitive to frost. Jícama also prefers full sun and rich, moist soil. Southern gardeners will have greater success with the plant than their northern counterparts, as it takes five to nine months to produce harvestable tubers from plants grown from seed. If you purchase jícamas for planting in the garden from your local Hispanic market (they are also increasingly available at larger supermarkets), buy the smallest ones you can find so you have the pleasure of planting them and growing them on. If you start plants from whole, small tubers you may be able to harvest mature roots after just three months or so. As the plant flowers, remove the blooms to encourage it to produce tubers. Under perfect growing conditions, including a long growing season, the tubers could grow to 5 or 6 feet in length and up to 50 pounds in weight; during most North American growing seasons, tubers will never get that large. In any case, Jícama tubers allowed to grow over 3 or 4 pounds will become unpleasantly woody and lose their appealing juicy crispness.

Hardiness USDA Zones 10 to 11

Propagation Jícama may be grown from seed in the warmest regions of the U.S., but most gardeners will get more satisfying results by planting small store-bought tubers in spring after danger of frost is past.

Cultivars and Related Species The tubers of *Pachyrhizus erosus* 'Mexican Turnip' are more oval (somewhat reminiscent of a sugar beet) than the typical flattened globe shape found in supermarkets. *Pachyrhizus tuberosus*, the Amazonian yam bean (known as jícama de leche in Spanish) is native to the headwaters of the Amazon and is cultivated in the Andes in Ecuador, as well as in the West Indies and China. Prepare it in the same fashion as jícama. *Pachyrhizus ahipa*, the Andean yam bean (commonly known as ahipa) is a more obscure species and may not be available in North America.

Cooking and Eating The white-fleshed, globe- or beet-shaped tubers can be eaten raw, stir-fried, boiled, roasted, braised, or simmered in soups. It is one of the few vegetables that remain crunchy even after cooking. Raw jícama is divine when sliced thinly and sprinkled with salt and ground chili pepper (see page 89). Jícama is also the source of a starch used in custards and puddings. Note that all above-ground plant parts are considered toxic, due to their high rotenone content.

Nutritional Value The jícama tuber is regarded as a healthy food because it contains up to 15 percent highly digestible carbohydrates, over 2 percent protein, and very little fat.

Pediomelum esculentum

Prairie Turnip, Indian Breadroot

The prairie turnip's many other common names—tipsin, teepsenee, breadroot, breadroot scurf pea, and pomme blanche—are evidence of its important place in North American prairie ethnobotany. It occurs throughout North Dakota and in the prairie region of Minnesota, and more rarely in the Southwest; its tubers played a valuable role in the diets of the Blackfoot, Cheyenne, Dakota, and Winnebago peoples (among others), who educated European explorers in its uses. Around 1800, settlers sent it back to Europe as a potential potato competitor, but it was not well received, and the plant remains uncultivated.

Ornamental Attributes This native perennial plant is most commonly found in prairies and dry woodlands of North Dakota and Wisconsin, southward to Missouri and Texas. It grows from sturdy brown roots that form 1½- to 4-inch-long, rounded tubers a few inches below the surface. The aboveground portion of prairie turnip is composed of several densely fuzzy stems that reach about a foot in height, bearing velvety compound leaves composed of tapered leaflets. In summer the plant produces abundant blue or purple flowers in clusters 2 to 4 inches long, followed by flattened, slender-tipped pods. In a prairie meadow, this would be a good multipurpose plant: attractive, nitrogen fixing, drought resistant, and edible.

Growing Tips The plant has a short season; it starts growing in May, flowers in June, and matures in July and August. Prairie turnip succeeds in ordi-nary but well-drained soil in a sunny spot. It is almost impossible to transplant seedlings without fatal damage to the root, so for the best success, plant the seeds in the ground in the spring after all danger of frost has passed. Cover them lightly with soil. Otherwise, in early to midspring, presoak the seeds for 24 hours in warm water, then sow in individual pots or a seed tray. Put these in a greenhouse or sunny, south-facing windowsill; to avoid disturbing the roots, pot up the young seedlings as soon as the first pair of true leaves appear. When transplanting, handle them with care: Use a plant label, tiny ice cream spoon, or chopstick to help you lift and transfer the seedlings to their new homes. Grow them in the pots until planting out in their final spot in the garden after the last frost date. Prairie turnip will not survive in areas with high moisture and humidity.

Propagation Prairie turnip does best started from seed. It is practically impossible to divide this perennial due to its finicky nature—the root rarely resprouts after tubers have been harvested—but you may succeed after some experimentation; harvest the tubers when the plant's seedpods are dry, and leave the plant tops and their seeds on the ground to germinate naturally.

Hardiness USDA Zones 4 to 11

Cultivars and Related Species None.

Cooking and Eating Prairie turnip forms rounded, carbohydrate-rich tubers with a flavor that has been likened to a sweet turnip. You can eat the starchy, glutinous root raw, boiled, baked, fried, or roasted. Prairie turnips can also be dried and stored for future use. Grind the dried tubers into flour and use it to enhance other foods, thicken soups, and to make bread and puddings.

Nutritional Value The tubers of prairie turnip contain furanocoumarins, substances that may cause heightened photosensitivity in some people.

Plectranthus esculentus

Livingstone Potato, Pomme de Terre d'Afrique (French), Tsenza (Shona)

The Livingstone potato—known as tsenza in Shona, the language of Zimbabwe—is one of the edible indigenous tuber crops once commonly grown in both the dryland and wetland areas of the eastern districts of Zimbabwe to Nigeria, south to Transvaal and Natal. Tsenza has been cultivated there since prehistoric times and is occasionally still seen in rural parts of southern Africa. It is also grown in Malaysia, Indonesia, and India. Although tsenza has been cultivated for millennia, it is considered one of the "lost" crops of Africa—scientists were not aware that it was still being cultivated until the mid-1960s. Tsenza could once again become an important tuber crop in rural Africa if its production was expanded. Despite its nutritional value and its acceptance there, though, it has received little or no attention from agricultural researchers.

Ornamental Attributes Livingstone potato grows to about 3 feet high and has an overall mintlike appearance. Both sides of the oval, puckered leaves are covered with short hairs. It would make an unusual and interesting addition to the fragrant herb or flower garden, potager, or annual border, planted near the edge where its foliage could be rubbed and sniffed. It rarely produces flowers, but when it does, they are small, yellow, and tubular. The fruit is a tiny, brown nutlet, which bears four extremely small seeds.

Growing Tips Livingstone potato is easy to grow in frost-free areas. It is worth experimenting with as far north as you can grow tomatoes. Plant seed tubers on mounds or hills (like regular potato), ridges, or rows, in well-drained soil in full sun after all danger of frost has passed and the soil is thoroughly warmed. Prepare the soil well to a depth of 1 foot before planting: Remove stones, crush large clods, and work in well-rotted manure or compost. Plant the tubers 2 to 4 inches deep and about 12 inches apart. If planting in rows, make them 2 to 3½ feet apart; if planting on ridges, make them 2 to 2½ feet apart. Mound up the soil around the shoots' bases to encourage the production of tubers. You can harvest these 180 to 200 days after planting by pulling up the plants with the tubers still attached. In northern zones try growing the plants in a large container outdoors in full sun in summer; move them indoors over the winter and keep them in a sunny greenhouse or bay window. Indoors, watch for mealy bugs and spider mites.

Propagation This plant is a cinch to propagate from cuttings, just like its basil, mint, and rosemary cousins. Try starting the tubers indoors or under glass in pots to get a jump-start on the growing season.

Hardiness USDA Zones 10 to 11

Cultivars and Related Species As of now, there are no cultivars.

Cooking and Eating This aromatic herb produces elongated white-, brown-, or black-skinned tubers from its shallow, fibrous root system. It is a member of the mint family, so the tubers have an aromatic, minty-oregano flavor. Tubers can grow to the thickness of a person's wrist but are usually much smaller. Use them as you would potatoes; wash them, then boil, roast, or bake them. They can be mashed, added to soups and stews, or fried like croquettes. Their minty flavor marries well with yogurt or sour cream.

Nutritional Value Livingstone potato has a high amino acid content and significant levels of calcium, iron, and vitamin A.

Sagittaria trifolia var. *sinensis*

Chinese Arrowhead, Tzi Koo (Chinese)

This arrowhead is a Chinese species, cultivated there and in Japan for its edible, starchy corms, which are produced in inundated soil on the ends of long stolons. The corms enable the plant to survive the cool, dry winter season and then grow very quickly when the summer monsoons come. Chinese arrowhead corms are traditionally eaten on Chinese New Year, sliced and stir-fried in hoisin sauce.

Ornamental Attributes *Sagittaria trifolia* var. *sinensis* is a member of a plant family found growing along muddy banks or in shallow water in temperate and tropical Europe, Asia, and the Americas. This species has lance- or arrowhead-shaped leaves (the genus name means "shaped like an arrowhead") 4 to 12 inches long. In summer it produces tall flower stems bearing whorls of small white flowers with a purple blotch at the base of each. All species of *Sagittaria* make handsome additions to a container water garden.

Growing Tips This plant has a tendency to spread, so container cultivation is recommended. Grow Chinese arrowhead in full to partial sun, paddy-style, under about 6 inches of water in a wading pool, salvaged cistern, half-barrel, or other watertight container in or above the ground. Chinese arrowhead corms are inexpensive and available in Asian markets from late fall through winter. Store them in damp sand until you are ready to plant them in spring. Plant them 2 to 3 inches deep in sandy loam or other soil substrate in full sun. Remove flower spikes as the plants produce them to increase corm formation. Chinese arrowhead is fairly cold tolerant and will survive chilly temperatures, though the top growth will die back once temperatures fall below freezing. Farther north, harvest the corms in fall when the foliage withers. The plant grows best in warm weather and requires at least a six-month growing season.

Propagation Runners can easily be transplanted anytime during the growing season. You can also plant corms purchased from Asian markets, and after the first harvest, reserve and store the smaller ones in damp sand for replanting in the spring after danger of frost has passed. Where growing seasons are less than six months, you can start them indoors in individual pots and transplant out.

Hardiness USDA Zones 7 to 11

Cultivars and Related Species *Sagittaria latifolia* (the broadleaf arrow-

head or wapatoo) is hardy in Zones 5 to 11. Native Americans ate them cooked in a number of ways, including with venison and maple syrup; they also sliced them and strung them on string (like dried apples) for winter use. Broadleaf arrowhead is popular with foragers, but it should only be collected in fall when the tubers are at their plumpest. Be sure the body of water from which they are gathered is unpolluted (For foraging guidelines, see page 97).

Cooking and Eating The edible corm is 2 inches across with a prominent growing tip and a light tan skin. The interior is off-white and the texture crisp. Peel and cut them up, then boil until tender, stir-fry, or slice and deep fry like potato chips.

To avoid freshwater-borne pathogens, never eat the tubers raw.

Nutritional Value The tubers have a high protein content for a root vegetable, up to 7 percent.

Smallanthus sonchifolius

Bolivian Sunroot, Yacón (Spanish)

Yacón is a Peruvian and Bolivian cousin of North America's Jerusalem artichoke, and like its northern relative, it is cultivated for its edible dahlia-like, irregular tubers. The plant was highly prized by the Incas, and remnants of it have been found at archaeological sites in coastal Peru. Ecuadoreans traditionally consume yacón during their Dia de Todos los Santos and Dia de los Muertos (All Saints and Day of the Dead) festivals. It is now being cultivated experimentally in New Zealand, where it is considered a gourmet vegetable.

Ornamental Attributes Yacón, which looks very much like Jerusalem artichoke, grows 3 to 9 feet tall and bears slightly furry, sticky foliage. The smallish daisy-shaped flowers range from bright yellow to orange. The flowers are great for late-summer arrangements.

Growing Tips Yacón adapts to a wide variety of soils but prefers a rich, moderately deep, light, well-drained soil in full sun. It has a wide pH tolerance, from acid to slightly alkaline. It is quite heat tolerant but very susceptible to cold; several hours at 32°F can kill all plant parts. Grow it as an annual in northern regions. Store autumn-dug tubers in slightly damp peat moss in a cool area for spring replanting. Water yacón regularly during dry spells.

Propagation Yacón is easily propagated using pieces of tuber. Before planting, rub the cut surfaces with a newly purchased cinnamon stick, an effective organic fungicide.

Hardiness USDA Zones 10 to 11

Cultivars and Related Species Although there are several varieties cultivated in the Andes, especially in southwestern Peru, only the straight species is available in the United States.

Cooking and Eating The outer coating of yacón (which is resinous and not edible) varies from brown to pink or purplish to cream or ivory. The interior is off-white, with a flavor very similar to that of the Jerusalem artichoke—crisp, crunchy, sweet, juicy, and delectable. Like Jerusalem artichokes, the sugar comes from inulin, not sucrose, making this an excellent food for diabetics. The tubers taste sweeter when they are allowed to cure in the sun after harvesting (or alternately left on a sunny windowsill indoors for a week or so), until the skins are slightly wrinkled. They can be eaten fresh out of hand, like fruit. They are wonderful as a salad when combined with carrots, raw sweet potatoes, and jícama; they also go nicely with fruit, especially sliced with bananas and oranges; and stewed. People in the Andes squeeze the grated pulp through a cloth to create a sweet, refreshing drink. They also cook the foliage like spinach.

Nutritional Value The tubers contain up to 2 percent protein, less than 1 percent fat, and fair amounts of calcium, phosphorous, and vitamin C.

Solanum jamesii

Colorado Wild Potato

The Colorado wild potato, native to the U.S. Southwest and Mexico, produces quite small, starch-rich tubers that range from pea- to walnut-sized. The Navajo, Tewa, Islet, Apache, and other southwestern tribes traditionally ate the tubers raw, boiled, or baked. The Hopi cook the tubers in saline clay and also use them to make yeast for bread baking. Australian agronomists are experimenting with *Solanum jamesii*, assessing its potential as a crop that can be grown on a large scale.

Ornamental Attributes *Solanum jamesii* is a herbaceous perennial that grows to about 1 foot tall. The insect-pollinated flowers have white petals and resemble tomato blossoms. Inedible, grape-sized berries follow them. The compound foliage is softly hairy, with 1½-inch, oval leaflets on leaves up to 4 inches long.

Growing Tips Yields are best in a slightly acid, fertile soil rich in organic matter, so amend your soil with plenty of compost or well-rotted manure. Colorado wild potatoes dislike wet or heavy clay soils. In limy soils or those low in humus, the tubers will be susceptible to scab. Sow seed in early spring in a warm greenhouse or on a sunny windowsill. Pot the seedlings into a fairly rich soil mixture as soon as they are large enough to handle; harden them off and set out after the last expected frost date. The tubers are somewhat labor intensive to harvest: They are small and often produced at the root tips, which may grow a good way from the parent plant. Harvest the tubers in autumn after frost has killed back the foliage. Store them in a cool, dark, frost-free place over the winter and replant in spring after all danger of frost has passed. In frost-free areas, you can leave them in the ground and treat them as perennials, but annual rejuvenation of the clumps may yield better results.

Propagation Start from seed or separate the tuber clusters and plant individually. Very large tubers can be cut into pieces and planted in the spring, much like seed potatoes.

Hardiness USDA Zones 9 to 11

Cultivars and Related Species None at the moment, but it warrants exploration for prospective future selections.

Cooking and Eating The starchy tubers are quite small, usually ranging in size from a pea to a walnut. They

have a bitterness that is concentrated near the skin; remove this before eating. Because of Colorado wild potatoes' slight alkaloid content, it is probably wiser not to eat them raw. Instead, peel the tubers, then bake or boil them. You can store them for several months or dry the tubers and then grind them into a flour to thicken soups and stews or to make bread. The tubers are lacking in gluten, which is found in true cereals and enables bread to rise. To make a workable dough, mix Colorado wild potato flour with wheat flour.

Nutritional Value This tuber is rich in carbohydrates and low in protein.

Solanum tuberosum

Potato, Papa (Spanish)

Seven thousand or more years ago, people living around Lake Titicaca in Bolivia and Peru developed the potato, an indigenous plant, as a crop, and it is still a major food source in that region. Hundreds of wild and semidomesticated types can be found there today. Spanish explorers brought potatoes back to Europe where they eventually became popular, first among hungry peasants and later among the poor and rich alike. By the mid-19th century, potatoes were the main and sometimes only food for millions of people throughout northern and central Europe, especially in Ireland and Holland. (Stamppot, mashed potatoes mixed with cooked cabbage, kale, or broccoli leaves, is a national dish in the Netherlands.) When the potato blight fungus hit Europe in the late 1840s, causing widespread crop failure, at least a million people died in Ireland of famine, and another 700,000 fled to the U.S. Nevertheless, potato cultivation continued to spread, and today, potatoes are a major staple food in all temperate regions.

Ornamental Attributes This familiar plant produces weak stems that emerge from the underground tubers. The compound leaves are slightly hairy. Attractive white to purple flowers are followed by grape-sized, poisonous fruit.

Growing Tips Growing potatoes at home is easy. They want a deeply dug, moisture-retentive but well-drained soil; a sandy loam is ideal. They require a fairly strict pH; 6.3 to 6.7 will do nicely. (In alkaline soils the tubers will develop scab.) A pound of seed potatoes will plant a row 8 to 10 feet long, with 12 inches between plants. When soil temperatures range from 55°F to 65°F, plant the seed potatoes 2 to 4 inches deep. When the top growth reaches 8 inches, cover the stems halfway up with soil, or mulch them to keep the roots cool. After about 40 to 60 days of growth, or when the plants are in flower, you can harvest small, new potatoes. Dig up your main potato harvest when the top growth withers in late summer or early fall, and the tubers have remained in the soil for two weeks, which "cures" or toughens the skin, aiding in avoiding damage.

Propagation Unlike most other vegetables, potatoes are not grown from seed but from small whole tubers (called seed potatoes) or portions of large ones.

Hardiness Grown as an annual.

Cultivars and Related Species There are innumerable potato cultivars, which are grouped by the number of growing days until harvest: early (55 to 65 days); midseason (70 to 80 days); and late (85 to 95 days). 'Yukon Gold' is extra early (about 55 days) and has smooth, thin, yellow skin and yellow flesh. Midseason 'Huckleberry' has maroon to beet-red skin and dark pink flesh with white marbling. 'Russet Burbank' is late (90 to 120 days) and considered the Idaho potato. The image below shows the cultivar 'Purple Viking'.

Cooking and Eating The potato is one of the most versatile of all vegetables and is used in a wide range of recipes. It can be boiled, baked, roasted, steamed, mashed, deep-fried, sautéed, or stewed in soups. The cooked skins can be eaten separately. Potatoes are used commercially to make starch, for distilling into alcohol (especially vodka and aquavit), and in baked goods. Because of their generally high alkaloid content, potatoes should not be eaten raw.

Nutritional Value The potato tuber is rich in carbohydrates, low in protein, and contains a fair amount of calcium, potassium, iron, and vitamin B.

Stachys affinis

Chinese Artichoke, Crosne (French)

Like the Livingstone potato (page 64), this unusual plant is a tuberous cousin of basil, rosemary, and thyme, and a member of the mint family. In China, its land of origin, *Stachys affinis* is called kam lu or "sweet pink" and tsao che tsan, "silkworm stone plant." To the Chinese and Japanese, this is an exceptionally special vegetable because of its likeness to pale jade when it is freshly dug. The plant's French name refers to the town Crosne, where the plants were first grown after their introduction to Europe in 1882. Since the 1990s they have been cultivated experimentally in Australia.

Ornamental Attributes *Stachys affinis* grows to about 18 inches tall and 10 inches wide. Like other members of the mint family, it has deep green, wrinkled, rough, and hairy foliage held on the square stems characteristic of this family. Plants produce spikes of tubular, two-lipped, white, pink, or lavender flowers from July to August. The handsome flowers are quite attractive to bees and butterflies, and they make terrific cut flowers.

Growing Tips In areas where Chinese artichoke is hardy, you can leave the tubers in the ground as a perennial root crop. Unlike other *Stachys* species, this one prefers a moist, rich, sandy soil with a limited pH range—6.6 to 7.5 (slightly acid to fairly neutral), and it dislikes a shortage of water, which prompts it to go dormant. Plant the tubers about 3 inches deep and 6 inches apart in early spring after all danger of frost has passed. Because the tubers are tiny, a large planting may be necessary. The plant prefers full sun but can take light shade and is very tolerant of high summer temperatures. Plants need five to seven months to develop tubers; harvest them after frost has killed the top growth or anytime during their dormancy, when the soil is easy to dig. (You can also replant the tubers during this time.)

Propagation Plants rarely set seed, but if you do obtain it, sow it in spring in a cold frame. Pot up the seedlings individually when they are large enough to handle, harden them off, and then plant out in your beds. Reserve tubers that are too small for the kitchen as starters for the following year's crop.

Hardiness USDA Zones 9 to 11

Cultivars and Related Species None. *Stachys affinis* would be a good candidate for a breeding and selection regi-

men; larger, smoother tubers are desirable qualities.

Cooking and Eating The pale tan tubers are 3 inches long and a half inch wide at their largest, with swollen, rounded, regularly spaced segments. The crisp, white flesh has a nutty, artichoke-like flavor. Because of their ridges these tubers are difficult to clean. Soak them first in a bucket of water to make the job easier. You can eat them raw, fried, roasted, steamed, boiled, or pickled. In Japan, they are pickled like ume plums in a mixture of salt and red shiso (*Perilla frutescens*) leaves. The tubers quickly discolor when exposed to air and are said to lose flavor when peeled.

Nutritional Value The starch of these low-calorie tubers is easily digested, and the protein content is considered rather high at about 25 percent.

Tropaeolum tuberosum

Tuberous Nasturtium, Añu, Mashua (Spanish)

Añu, a cousin of the popular garden nasturtium *Tropaeolum majus*, has been cultivated for its edible tubers since about 5500 B.C. Pre-Incan people drew pictograms of the tubers in the mountains of the high Andes, and añu remains an important crop among the Andean people of Bolivia, Peru, Ecuador, Colombia, and Venezuela.

Ornamental Attributes Añu vine clambers to about 6 feet tall. Like the familiar garden nasturtium, the tuberous nasturtium's scalloped foliage is attached to the leaf stalk in the center of the leaf. Its spurred, orange to scarlet flowers are far narrower in shape than the common garden type, but plants produce them freely throughout the summer. Provide the plants with a trellis or other support on which to climb to their full height. Añu would also be an unusual—and useful—alpine or rock garden plant, but it doesn't perform well in warm, humid climates.

Growing Tips Añu is typically a short-day plant in northern latitudes and will not set flowers and tubers until after the middle of September, when days are markedly shorter. Start plants in early spring and grow as long as possible before frost hits in order to harvest a serviceable crop. Plant the tubers or seeds as soon as it has warmed up thoroughly in a loose, moderately fertile, well-drained soil with a pH between 5.3 and 7.5. Plants require water throughout the growing season and will die back if they dry out. Grow them in containers in a cool greenhouse using bulb pans or azalea pots; watch for mealy bugs, spider mites, and white flies if you grow them indoors. Harvest the tubers after the foliage is killed by the first hard frost.

Propagation Grow añu from seed planted indoors in early spring; from tubers harvested the previous autumn and stored in a cool place until spring; and from basal-stem cuttings.

Hardiness USDA Zones 3 to 6

Cultivars and Related Species The short-day cultivar *Tropaeolum tuberosum* 'Miuri' produces white tubers mottled with purple. 'Ken Aslet', which bears yellowish tubers attractively splashed with crimson, is day-neutral and begins to flower from July onward.

Cooking and Eating Tuberous nasturtium produces its elongated, slightly rough tubers at the ends of underground stems. Their skin varies from white to yellow to an occasional purple or red and is often striped or mottled red or purple, especially underneath the eyes. Their flesh is yellow. Freezing or drying the tubers before cooking is said to mellow and improve their flavor, which is peppery. Boil the tubers for about ten minutes before serving them as a vegetable or adding them to stews. They are often frozen after being boiled, and in this form are considered an icy delicacy. The young shoots and flowers are edible as well.

Nutritional Value The tubers contain 10 percent carbohydrates, up to 2 percent protein (although some Andean selections contain up to 11 percent protein), and are rich in vitamin C. They also contain the same sharp-tasting mustard oils as the unrelated mustard and horseradish.

Typha latifolia

Broadleaf Cattail

This North American aquatic plant was extensively used by Native Americans across the continent: People including the Iroquois and Cherokee in the East, the Sioux, Osage, and Blackfeet in the Midwest, the Apache and Navaho of the Southwest, and the Northern and Southern Paiute and Chinookan tribes in the West employed everything from its rhizomatous roots to its pollen and flower spikes for food, medicine, and shelter. The plant's starchy rhizomes were boiled, roasted, baked, or dried and pulverized into flour for porridge and mush, especially when other foods were scarce.

Ornamental Attributes Members of the genus *Typha* form dense, robust stands of vegetation around the edges of lakes, ponds, and slow-moving streams. Broadleaf cattail produces strap-shaped leaves to 6 feet long, and in summer it bears dark brown flower spikes 6 to 9 inches long. The decorative catkins are lovely cut and used in dried arrangements, or they can be left standing for winter interest. They are quite aggressive growers in earth-bottomed bodies of fresh water and can become a nuisance.

Growing Tips Broadleaf cattail should be planted in moist soils in natural ponds or in large containers filled with soil and inundated with water in late fall to give the plant's root system to get established before heavy flooding and winter dormancy set in. If you are growing cattail in containers, wait for spring to plant. Cattail will survive best if plants are dormant when

planted and if the soil is moist. The rhizomes can form large intertwined masses 2 to 6 inches under the surface at the bottom of ponds. Harvest the rhizomes in early spring before growth begins or in autumn after the foliage has died down; at these times the rhizomes are plump and chock-full of carbohydrates as they prepare to go into or come out of dormancy.

Propagation Grow broadleaf cattail from rhizomes or from seed planted indoors in early spring in moist but not soggy soil.

Hardiness USDA Zones 3 to 11

Cultivars and Related Species The one available cultivar, *Typha latifolia* 'Variegata', is much less vigorous than the species. Its leaves have longitudinal cream stripes, and it grows to 3 to 4 feet tall.

Cooking and Eating The broadleaf cattail's ropelike tan or reddish-brown,

starchy rhizomes are about an inch thick and up to several feet long. The plant's rhizomes and its lateral shoots, leaf shoots, pollen, and flower spikes are all edible. Carefully clean off the mud, then peel or scrape off the skin to reveal the tough, white inner core—which may be eaten raw, baked, roasted, or broiled. (If the core is brownish, it is rotten and not edible.) You can also make flour: Smash the peeled rhizomes and soak them in water to separate out the stringy pith, which you remove. Finely strain the remaining pulp in a couple of changes of water and dry before grinding. Some people use the pollen as a flour supplement (substituting as much as half of the volume of wheat flour in a recipe). Boil the young green flowering stalks and nibble them like sweet corn on the cob (plenty of butter helps).

Nutritional Value Cattail rhizomes are high in starch, about 30 to 46 percent.

Ullucus tuberosus

Ulluco (Spanish)

Along with potatoes, añu, and oca, ulluco has been an important root crop in the Andes for millennia. It is cultivated from Colombia south to northern Argentina and is the hardiest of the Andean crops (its top growth survives temperatures to about 29°F). Ceremonial vessels of the Wari culture (approximately 500 to 1000 A.D.) have been found decorated with multicolored representations of Andean plants, including ulluco. In the cold altiplano areas of the Andes the plant's tubers are frozen and then dried. The resulting product is called chuño, a name first used for dried potatoes but now used for any dehydrated vegetable. Its leaves are eaten raw in salads or cooked like a potherb. The tubers can be found in Hispanic markets, and canned ulluco has become an important Peruvian export product. The plant is also being grown experimentally as a root crop in New Zealand.

Ornamental Attributes Ulluco is a perennial herb with heart-shaped, fleshy, hairless foliage and tiny pinkish-yellow flowers followed by tiny berries.

Growing Tips Ulluco requires full sun and a light, rich, well-drained soil with a pH ranging from 5.5 to 6.5. Plants produce tubers both on the above-ground stems at the leaf axils as well as underground. Like oca, it does not produce tubers until the short days of autumn, when the day length is reduced to about nine hours. The plant needs seven to eight months of frost-free growing time until harvest. In some areas, slugs can be a problem. North of Zone 7 cultivate ulluco in containers and overwinter it in a cool greenhouse or alpine house.

Propagation Ulluco is grown like potato, from whole or cut tubers (see page 73).

Hardiness USDA Zones 7 to 10

Cultivars and Related Species Several Andean cultivars may only be available south of the border or from Australian or New Zealand specialty houses. *Ullucus tuberosus* 'Plata de Monte' produces smooth, medium-sized, roundish tubers with a glossy white skin occasionally mottled with pink. 'Shrimp of the Earth' has small, curved tubers with bright pinkish-maroon skin, somewhat reminiscent of its cultivar name. (This form is highly desirable in the Andes and commands a high price.) 'Yellow Jewels', with soft, pastel-yellow tubers, is a very high-quality strain with good form, size, and uniformity.

Cooking and Eating Ulluco produces its subterranean tubers at the ends of slender roots. The tubers are 2 to 3 inches long and round or elongated (very much like "new" potatoes), with skin that varies from white to yellow, pink, red, or purple, depending on the strain. The interior is white with a usually crisp texture, though some types are soft. The major appeal of ulluco is this crisp texture, which, like that of jícama, remains even when the tubers are cooked. The tubers are traditionally boiled and served with vinegar—an Andean version of German potato salad! When boiled and fried (they are rarely baked because of their high water content), they taste like potatoes. They may also be added to soups and stews as a thickening agent.

Nutritional Value Fresh tubers contain 12 to 14 percent starch and up to 2 percent protein, as well as vitamin C, calcium, and carotene.

Xanthosoma sagittifolium

New Cocoyam, Tannia, Yautía (Spanish)

Yautía is the New World's answer to the Old World's significant crop taro (*Colocasia esculenta*, page 36). Like taro, yautía is an agriculturally important aroid. It has been cultivated in tropical South America and the Caribbean (where the Taino and Arawak Indians relied on it) since pre-Columbian times. During the 16th and 17th centuries, slave traders introduced it into West Africa. It became popular there, mainly because it's perfect for the traditional African dish fufu (originally made from yams), in which cooked tubers are ground into a paste, rolled into balls, and eaten out of hand or like dumplings in soups and stews. It also proved to be more robust and disease resistant in adverse conditions than taro, tolerating a certain amount of drought and shade and giving heavier yields on drier soils—and it can also be grown on land that is too wet for yams but not wet enough for taro. For these reasons it has become an important crop in Africa.

Ornamental Attributes Yautía can reach 6 feet in height and bears 3-foot-long, arrowhead-shaped foliage. It lends a tropical air to any landscape—the often silver-streaked foliage is exceptionally stunning.

Growing Tips Yautía likes either full sun or partial shade and a rich, neutral to slightly acid, moisture-retentive soil; it dislikes waterlogged conditions. Plants need almost a year to produce a serviceable harvest, although small rhizomes can be "robbed" from the still-intact parent plant every three to six months after the first planting. In northern locales, grow the plants in large containers, moving to larger pots frequently to accommodate their rapid growth. Water frequently and apply a water-soluble organic fertilizer every three weeks. Overwinter them in a sunny greenhouse or bay window and watch for spider mites and mealy bugs. You can also dry out the plant a little by withholding water, then lift the rhizomes and store them in moist sand in a cool but frost-free area until spring. The plants are grown from tubers (those procured from an ethnic market usually work well and are inexpensive). For a photo of the tuber, see page 7.

Propagation Propagate new plants by replanting offsets from the tubers.

Hardiness USDA Zones 10 to 11

Cultivars and Related Species Hispanic and Asian markets in the U.S. almost always offer the straight *Xanthosoma* species. Collections in

Puerto Rico, Trinidad, and Tobago, though, describe 40 or more *Xanthosoma* cultivars, displaying a wide variety of habit and leaf shape.

Cooking and Eating The tubers, stems, and young leaves are all edible. The globe-shaped or cylindrical potato-sized corms have white, pink, or yellow flesh and pale brown skin with prominent leaf scars. This plant is an aroid and should never be eaten raw. Like *Alocasia*, all parts of this plant contain calcium oxalate, making it not only bitter and unpleasant tasting when uncooked but also the source of intense discomfort to unwary samplers—as if thousands of needles are piercing the lips, mouth, and throat—when even the tiniest amount is chewed raw. The tubers have an earthy, nutty flavor and are peeled (wear gloves if you have sensitive skin) and then eaten boiled, baked, puréed, simmered in soups and stews, or made into chips, pancakes, fufu, or fritters (see page 94 for a recipe). The plant's young leaves and petioles are boiled and eaten like spinach.

Nutritional Value Yautía is high in carbohydrates and contains 2 to 3 percent protein as well.

Dong Rieng, canna starch noodle salad from Vietnam.

Cooking With Tubers

Scott D. Appell

Cooks around the world rely on tubers, corms, and rhizomes as an integral part, if not sole constituent, of daily meals. Undemanding to cultivate in the home garden, simple to find in the wild, or easily procured in local markets, they prove filling, nutritious, wildly versatile, and affordable foodstuffs.

The recipes offered here range the globe—and many of the ingredients may be initially unfamiliar. The more common ones (such as Jerusalem artichokes or 'Yukon Gold' potatoes) are generally available at large supermarkets, but others, like jícama, taro, and yautía, haven't made it into the mainstream yet and may require a trip to a specialty food store or an ethnic market.

Don't hesitate to experiment; try substituting one tuber or cooking technique for another (keeping in mind that some tubers must be cooked before eating). After all, necessity is the mother of invention.

All-Purpose Tuber Gratin
Tubereux Gratinés Jurassiens | Tuber Gratin, France

2 pounds tubers (such as potatoes, taro, yautía, sweet potatoes, yacón, oca,
   or Jerusalem artichokes)

1 cup parmesan or gruyere cheese, grated

1¼ cups heavy cream

1 stick unsalted butter (¼ pound)

Salt

Freshly ground black pepper

Preheat oven to 300°F. Butter a 10-by-10-inch, 2-inch-deep fireproof dish. Tubers with particularly coarse, thick, or hairy skin (such as aroids and yuca) should be peeled. For large tubers such as potatoes, taro, yautía, sweet potatoes, or yacón, slice into ⅛-inch slices to make 6 to 7 cups. Leave small tubers such as oca, Livingstone potatoes, and spring beauties whole. Arrange the tubers in layers in the buttered dish, seasoning each layer with salt, pepper, grated cheese, and dots of butter. End with a sprinkling of cheese and dots of butter. Pour the cream over the tubers and place the dish in the middle of the oven for 1 to 1¼ hours, regulating the temperature so that the cream never quite boils. The gratin is done when the tubers are tender and have absorbed the cream and the top is lightly browned. Serves 6.

Canna (*Canna edulis*)
Dong Rieng | Canna Starch Noodle Salad, Vietnam

6 to 8 ounces canna starch noodles (sometimes sold as cellophane noodles)

6 tablespoons dry-roasted peanuts, chopped

2 cups English cucumber, peeled and grated

2 cups carrot, peeled and grated

4 hard-boiled eggs, peeled and quartered

¼ cup fresh cilantro, chopped

¼ cup fresh large-leaf basil, chopped

Dressing

⅔ cup fresh lime juice (about 3 large limes)

½ cup hoisin sauce

(Continued)

- 1 ½ tablespoons granulated sugar
- 1 ¼ teaspoons crushed red pepper flakes
- 4 cloves garlic, finely minced

Cook the noodles according to package directions, drain, and place in a medium bowl. Whisk together the dressing ingredients and toss with the warm noodles. Transfer the noodles to a serving bowl, sprinkle with chopped peanuts, and chill before serving. On a large platter, arrange in a decorative fashion the cucumber, carrot, boiled eggs, cilantro, and basil. Guests can serve themselves a portion of noodles and assemble their salad as they like. Serves 4 to 6.

Chinese Water Chestnut
(*Eleocharis dulcis*)
Chow Faan Ma Tai | Fried Rice With Chinese Water Chestnuts, China

- 2 eggs
- ⅛ teaspoon ground white pepper
- 2 tablespoons toasted sesame oil
- ⅛ cup soy sauce
- ⅛ cup peanut oil
- 4 cups cold, cooked short-grain rice
- 2 tablespoons fresh ginger, finely chopped
- 2 cloves garlic, finely chopped
- 1 cup fresh Chinese water chestnuts, peeled and julienned
- 6 scallions (including green part), thinly sliced

Gently beat together the eggs, white pepper, sesame oil, and soy sauce and set aside. Heat a wok until hot and add the peanut oil and rice. Stir-fry the rice for several seconds, breaking up any lumps. Add the ginger and garlic and toss for 2 to 3 minutes. Add the water chestnuts and scallions and toss until heated through. Add the egg mixture and continue tossing until the eggs are just set. Serves 3 to 4.

Chow faan ma tai, fried rice with Chinese water chestnuts.

Dahlia (*Dahlia* hybrids)
Dahlia Tuber Quick Bread, United States)

2 large eggs	1 ½ teaspoon ground cinnamon
1 ½ teaspoon vanilla extract	Zest of 1 orange, chopped fine
1 cup vegetable or hazelnut oil	Zest of 1 lemon, chopped fine
1 cup granulated sugar	2 to 3 medium dahlia tubers, firm
1 ½ cups all-purpose flour	and unblemished
½ teaspoon baking powder	½ cup mini-chocolate or -carob chips
½ teaspoon baking soda	½ cup walnuts or hazelnuts, toasted
½ teaspoon salt	and chopped

Preheat oven to 350°. Grease a 9-by-5-inch loaf pan, line the bottom with greased waxed paper or parchment paper, and set aside. Whisk lightly together the eggs, vanilla extract, and oil, and set aside. In another bowl whisk together the sugar, flour, baking powder, baking soda, salt, cinnamon, and citrus zest. Peel and grate the dahlia tubers using a hand grater or the grater attachment of a food processor to make 1 cup of grated tubers. Working quickly, fold the liquid ingredients into the dry ingredients until just combined. Add the grated tubers, chocolate chips, and nuts. Immediately pour the batter into the prepared pan and bake for about 1 hour, or until a cake tester or wooden skewer inserted into the middle of the loaf comes out clean. Cool on a wire rack several minutes before unmolding onto the rack to cool completely. This quick bread freezes well wrapped in several layers of plastic wrap. Serves 4 to 6.

Jerusalem Artichoke
(*Helianthus tuberosus*)
Native American–Style Braised Jerusalem Artichokes, North America

2 pounds Jerusalem artichokes, well scrubbed

¼ cup bacon drippings or hazelnut oil

3 cups meat or vegetable stock

¼ cup freshly chopped sage leaves

1 teaspoon Mexican oregano

3 tablespoons wild onion greens or chives

4 or 5 juniper berries

Crushed sea salt

1 cup wild mushrooms, sliced

½ cup hazelnuts, toasted and chopped

Cut the Jerusalem artichokes into large, uniform chunks. In a heavy skillet heat the bacon drippings. Add the tubers and sauté over medium heat for several minutes. Add the stock, sage leaves, Mexican oregano, onion, juniper berries, and sea salt to taste. Cook 10 minutes, stirring occasionally, adding more stock as needed. Add the mushrooms and continue cooking until the tubers are knife tender but not mushy, 35 to 60 minutes in all. Transfer to a serving dish and sprinkle with chopped nuts. Serves 6.

Jícama (*Pachyrhizus erosus*)

Ensalada de Jícama Cruda | Jícama Salad, Mexico

2 medium jícamas (about 1 pound)

1 fresh red chile pepper, seeded and
   finely chopped

4 Key limes

Coarse sea salt

4 cups dandelion greens or escarole

Mexican ensalada de jícama cruda, jícama salad.

Scrub, peel, and slice the jícama into matchsticks and toss in a mixing bowl with sea salt and chile pepper to taste. Squeeze and strain one or two Key limes and toss the juice with the jícama. Chill before serving over the salad greens and garnish with additional lime wedges. Serves 4 to 6.

Sacred Lotus (*Nelumbo nucifera*)

Renkon Sunomono | Lotus Salad, Japan

Dressing

- 2 teaspoons mirin (sweet rice wine)
- 1 tablespoon light soy sauce
- 2 teaspoons wasabi paste
- ¼ cup rice wine vinegar
- 3 tablespoons sugar
- 1 tablespoon toasted sesame oil
- 2 tablespoons sesame seeds
- 2 lotus rhizomes, peeled and sliced ⅛-inch thick

Whisk together the dressing ingredients and set aside. Prepare the lotus rhizomes by washing them, trimming off the ends, and peeling them. Slice them and place in a bowl of ice water until ready to cook. Place the slices in one layer on the rack(s) of a steamer, set over boiling water, and cover. Steam 3 to 4 minutes, then remove and refresh under cold water. While the lotus is still warm, gently toss with the dressing. Chill before serving. Serves 3 to 4.

Sweet Corn Root (*Calathea allouia*)

Lerenes Hervidos | Buttered Sweet Corn Root, Puerto Rico

1 pound sweet corn roots	Fine sea salt
1 to 2 tablespoons butter	Freshly ground black pepper

See page 55 for a description of this root. Thoroughly rinse the sweet corn roots to remove soil and boil in about 6 cups of salted water until tender (50 to 60 minutes). When cool enough to handle, peel and serve them with melted butter, sea salt, and black pepper to taste. Serves 6.

Renkon sunomono, lotus salad from Japan.

Taro, *Colocasia esculenta,* in its raw form.

Sweet Potato (*Ipomoea batatas*)

Getuk Lindri | Sweet Potato Cakes, Indonesia

In many cultures in which the sweet potato is a staple, the white-fleshed form is preferred for its starchiness—but you can use any color in this recipe.

2 pounds sweet potatoes

2 ounces gula Jawa (block sugar
   made from the nectar of coconut
   palm flowers), grated, or light
   brown sugar

6 tablespoons coconut milk

2 ounces fresh coconut, grated

Salt

Wash and quarter the sweet potatoes and boil them until knife tender. Drain and skin them, then mash until smooth. Combine the gula Jawa and coconut milk in a small saucepan and heat until the gula Jawa is dissolved; remove from heat and let cool slightly before mixing into the mashed sweet potatoes. Force the mixture through a ricer onto parchment paper or a nonstick pan liner. Shape the strands into little lozenge shapes, 3 by 2 inches, and arrange on a serving plate. Mix the coconut with a pinch of salt and sprinkle it over the cakes before serving. Serves 4 to 6.

Taro (*Colocasia esculenta*)
West African–Style Honey-Roasted Taro, Africa

- **2 pounds taro roots of similar size**
- **Salt**
- **½ cup acacia honey**
- **½ cup raw peanuts**
- **4 tablespoons palm oil**

Preheat oven to 350°F. Blanch the well-scrubbed taro roots in boiling salted water for 15 minutes; then drain and refresh under cold water and peel when cool enough to handle. Cut the taro into fairly large pieces and toss with the honey, peanuts, and palm oil. Place the taro on a nonstick baking sheet and roast, turning frequently, until the tubers are knife tender. Serve hot. Serves 6.

Yam (*Dioscorea alata*)
Elizabeth Raffald's Yam Pudding, England

This 1769 recipe by Elizabeth Raffald (1733–1781) is presumed to be the earliest yam recipe included in an English cookery book. Mrs. Raffald was a pioneer among women entrepreneurs: She had a cooked-meat shop, wrote the first street directory, and ran an employment agency for servants, among other accomplishments. This sweet pudding is probably based on a recipe for sweet potato (*Ipomaea batatas*), which arrived in England before the yam. At that time sugar was considered a luxury food, and its use implied wealth. This dish would have been served with roast game or other meat. A modernized version of her recipe follows the original.

Take a middling white yam, and either boil it or roast it, then pare off the skin and pound it very fine, with three-quarters of a pound of butter, half a pound of sugar, a little mace, cinnamon, and twelve eggs, leaving out half the whites, beat them with a little rose water. You may put in a little citron cut small if you like it, and bake it nicely.

1 medium or 2 small yams (3 pounds)	2 tablespoons rose water
3 sticks unsalted butter, softened	1 tablespoon lemon zest, grated
1 cup sugar	$\frac{1}{2}$ teaspoon salt
1 teaspoon ground mace	5 large eggs
1 teaspoon ground cinnamon	5 large egg yolks

Preheat oven to 350°F. Boil the yams until tender, then drain, cool, and peel them. Thoroughly mash the yams, mixing in the butter as you go. Beat in the sugar, spices, rose water, lemon zest, and salt. In a separate bowl, beat together the whole eggs and egg yolks (reserve the extra whites for another use) until fluffy. Fold the eggs into the yam mixture and pour into a buttered, 3-quart soufflé dish. Bake until a cake tester or wooden skewer inserted into the center of the pudding comes out clean, about 35 to 40 minutes. Serves 6.

Yautía (*Xanthosoma sagittifolium*)

Frituras de Yautía y Queso Parmesano | Yautía and Parmesan Fritters, Puerto Rico

1½ pounds yautía, peeled and grated (about 3 cups)	1¼ teaspoon salt
⅓ cup parmesan cheese, freshly grated	2 tablespoons melted lard, bacon drippings, or olive oil
	Oil for frying

Mix together the yautía, cheese, salt, and melted lard. Form each fritter using 2 tablespoons of the mixture and place on a sheet of greased wax paper until ready to cook. In a deep skillet, fry the fritters in hot oil in a single, uncrowded layer, 4 minutes on each side or until golden brown. Remove and drain on absorbent paper. Serve warm as an appetizer or side dish. Serves 4 to 6.

Potatoes Versus Rice

James J. Lang

The lowly potato is far and away the world's most successful, productive, and nutritious tuber, and after rice, wheat, and corn it is the world's top crop. But is it as productive as the grains? And is it really any good to eat?

Let's compare potatoes with rice. Worldwide, farmers produce 618 million metric tons of paddy rice on 154 million hectares for a yield of 4 metric tons per hectare. By contrast, farmers grow 323 million tons of potatoes on just 18 million hectares for an overall yield of 18 metric tons per hectare. Even when the dry matter content—the edible portion—of each is calculated (a fresh potato is roughly 23 percent dry matter and 77 percent water; uncooked rough rice is about 86 percent dry matter and 14 percent water), the potato still comes out ahead. Worldwide, average production from a hectare of potatoes is 4.1 metric tons of dry matter (18 metric tons per hectare multiplied by 23 percent dry matter), compared with 3.4 metric tons for rice (4 metric tons per hectare multiplied by 86 percent dry matter). Western Australia has the highest potato yields in the world—an incredible 100

Good news for spud lovers: Potatoes are not just pretty and delicious, they are also economical; easy to grow, harvest, and prepare; and highly nutritious.

metric tons per hectare under irrigation, which translates into 23 metric tons of dry matter.

The potato also has an enviable harvest index—the ratio of the weight of usable food to the weight of the entire plant. Potatoes typically have a harvest index of between 75 and 85 percent, which means less than a fourth of what a potato plant makes out of sunlight, water, and nutrients is used for stems and leaves. The rest is food in tuber form. The harvest index for rice rarely exceeds 50 percent. It is also worth noting that a potato patch is much easier to plant than a rice field: All a farmer needs is a spade. By contrast, the work required to puddle and plant a rice paddy makes it a much more labor-intensive crop.

Potato Facts The potato may be more productive than rice, but surely it is not very nutritious. Wrong! Polished rice is notoriously deficient in vitamins. And whether polished or not, rice contains no vitamin C or A. By comparison, 100 grams of potato boiled fresh in its skin contains 6 to 12 milligrams of vitamin C, enough to prevent scurvy. The vitamin C in two fresh potatoes is equivalent to that in an orange. Eat 4 or 5 small boiled spuds and you will get all the vitamin C and potassium needed for the day.

Potatoes are also rich in the B complex vitamins. Eaten regularly, they have enough niacin (B5) to prevent pellagra and skin disorders; they are a good source of vitamin B6, thiamine (B1), and riboflavin (B2). Eaten with their skins on, potatoes provide dietary fiber; in fact, they have more fiber than rice.

When it comes to protein, potatoes do fall behind the grains: just 2.1 grams in 100 grams of fresh, uncooked spuds. Still, potato protein is rich in amino acids.

Potatoes also contain essential minerals, notably calcium, iron, phosphorus, and potassium. Based on comparable edible portions, potatoes have three times as much calcium and minerals as rice. Low in sodium, but rich in potassium and alkaline salts, potatoes qualify for salt-free diets and help reduce stomach acidity. Add in a little milk, and one can live indefinitely on potatoes, a claim neither rice nor wheat can match.

The problem with the potato is that it makes you fat, right? Wrong again! The potato has so little fat it should be labeled "fat free." The fat content of a fresh tuber is just two tenths of one percent. By comparison, wheat and rice seem like fatty foods; even a carrot has more fat than a potato. As for calories, a medium-sized potato has approximately 100 calories, comparable with a medium-sized pear. (I stake this claim on the baked, microwaved, or boiled spud—without butter, sour cream, or melted cheese.) The potato is filling, virtually fat free, low in calories, and low in cholesterol. It doesn't have much sugar, either; only about one percent of the dry matter in a potato is sucrose.

Finally, the nutritious yummy potato can be cooked in more ways than rice, and it can be converted into many versatile delicacies. Dig in!

Foraging for Wild Tubers

Leda Meredith

Wild-growing edible tubers and roots once provided supplemental food for people during times of plenty and could make the difference between survival and starvation in times of want. While sustenance is no longer an issue today in North America, plant conservation certainly is. These days, wild collection of many native species is controversial due to issues of sustainability and uncertainty about the long-term viability of indigenous plant populations. In any case, it's not really necessary to harvest native edibles in the wild when most of them can be grown at home as a renewable delight.

But if you decide to try foraging, find out if a plant is endangered in your state before you go picking or digging. Check the U.S. Department of Agriculture Natural Resources Conservation Service database of threatened and endangered plants online at http://plants.usda.gov/threat.html. Click on your state to select the relevant list by common or botanical name. Once you've determined that it's legal to take a plant from the wild, harvesting sustainably becomes top priority. Never take so much of any single plant population that it can't regenerate. A useful rule of thumb is to take at most ten percent of the plants from any one thriving patch of a species. If you find just a few plants, leave them alone. Instead, find out if the plant that you covet is being grown in cultivation. If it is, acquire it from a reputable nursery that propagates its own stock, plant it in your yard, and harvest as soon as your patch is large enough to sustain itself.

On many public lands the collection of plants is prohibited. Be sure you know the rules before you go foraging. Also bear in mind that a species may be plentiful in one area but absent or under protected status elsewhere.

Gather wild Jerusalem artichokes in late fall after a few hard frosts. Cold temperatures help convert some of the tubers' starch to sugar, making them sweet and crunchy.

Wild-growing edible tubers can be quite tricky to locate because the prime harvesting season for many of them is late fall through early spring—just when there are few to no leaves or flowers by which to identify the plants. It's often helpful to first identify the plants during their flowering season and get an idea of the size of a colony, and then come back later in the year to collect a few tubers.

Always be 100 percent certain of your identification, and verify it with a detailed field guide such as *Peterson's Field Guide to Edible Wild Plants* (Houghton Mifflin, 1999) or Steve Brill's *Identifying and Harvesting Wild Edible and Medicinal Plants* (William Morrow Publishers, 1994) or with a foraging expert. If in doubt, leave it out! Some of the choicest wild edibles grow side by side with poisonous look-alikes. For example, delicious sego lily (*Calochortus* species) bulbs are often found growing right next to the poisonous death camass (*Zigadenus* species). Don't be tempted, even if you can tell them apart. Consider the camass as a sort of bodyguard for the sego lilies, which should never be taken from the wild.

With underground crops, it is even more important than with other wild edibles to be mindful of contamination with pesticides, herbicides, and other chemicals because roots and other underground plant parts tend to collect more toxins than those aboveground. Suburban lawns are among the places most likely to be affected by this hazard, so if collecting from a neighbor's yard, always ask if nonorganic herbicides or pesticides have been used. If the answer is yes, pass up the opportunity to harvest there. Also, do not harvest within 50 feet of heavily trafficked roads. This is a sound rule not only because plants and soil may be contaminated with lead and other heavy metals from exhaust fumes but also because roadsides are often sprayed with chemicals.

On the next few pages you will find portraits of three tuberous plants that are widespread in the U.S. and Canada and are easy to identify correctly. (Two are nonnative weeds, so harvesting serves a dual purpose.) Needless to say, all three are delicious.

Cyperus esculentus
Nutsedge, Earth Almond, Tiger Nut, Chufa (Portuguese and Spanish)

Nutsedge has a long history of cultivation beginning 4,000 years ago in ancient Egypt. From there it made its way throughout the Middle East. In the Middle Ages, the Moors introduced nutsedge into Spain, and from there it was introduced to West Africa, India, and Brazil. The Costanoan, Paiute, Pomo, and Kashaya peoples of coastal areas of California and Oregon ate the almond-flavored tubers both raw and cooked. Though considered a native plant in North America, it has spread to regions outside its original range, and in many areas it has become an agricultural weed.

This grasslike plant bears slender, tapering foliage and yellow

Edible weeds like nutsedge, Cyperus esculentus, can be harvested with abandon.

to brown, spikelike flower parts held upon 2½-foot stems. The primary identification trait for this plant is the triangular shape of its stems. Nutsedge grows in full sun and moist to wet soil of average fertility. It is highly invasive and practically impossible to eradicate once introduced. The nutty tubers are round, oval, or lozenge-shaped and approximately the size of a chickpea. The skin of the tubers is light brown, the interior white.

Like its cousin Chinese water chestnut (*Eleocharis dulcis*, page 42), nutsedge remains crisp even when it's cooked. The tender tubers can be eaten raw, boiled, or roasted. They can be used in savory dishes, such as soups and stews, or in sweet recipes like cookies, puddings, and ice creams. The most famous preparation of *Cyperus esculentus* is the Spanish beverage horchata de chufa. It is made by soaking the crushed tubers in water, straining out the solids, and adding cinnamon, sugar, vanilla, and crushed ice. In some areas people roast the tubers, then grind them and use them as a caffeine-free coffee substitute. Both the "coffee" and the horchata are good ways to make use of those tubers that are too fibrous to enjoy eating whole.

Helianthus tuberosus
Jerusalem Artichoke, Sunchoke

Jerusalem artichokes are native to the Midwest but can be found throughout North America in sunny, dry locations. The rough stems of this native North American plant can grow as high as 10 feet, and the flowers and leaves resemble those of its cousin the common sunflower.

Overharvesting is seldom a concern with hardy Jerusalem artichoke: Even a small chunk of one of the tubers left in the ground produces a robust plant the following year, hence the traditional warning to plant them where you would like your grandchildren's grandchildren to harvest them. The tubers take some digging to get at, with the largest usually located one to two feet underground. However, each plant can yield two or more pounds of tubers, making it well worth the effort. The tubers can be unpleasantly musky because of their high inulin content. Cold weather converts some of this indigestible starch into natural sugars, so harvest Jerusalem artichoke after several hard frosts. Frost-treated tubers are sweet and crunchy raw and pleasantly earthy tasting cooked. They do not store well, and the best way to keep them for long periods is to leave them in the ground and dig them up as needed whenever the soil is not frozen.

The best time to forage is not always the best time to find the plants. Look for Jerusalem artichokes when they are in flower, and come back in late fall to dig up some tubers.

Hemerocallis fulva
Tawny Daylily

Originally from Eurasia and China, this vigorously growing plant was introduced into North America centuries ago as an ornamental and has subsequently escaped and naturalized. Tawny daylily can form huge colonies along roadsides, woodland edges, and abandoned fields and farmsteads from New England south to northern Florida. Although a breathtaking early-summer sight en masse, this plant is considered an invasive species, so collecting "wild" plants may actually be beneficial for the environment. Tawny daylily has straplike leaves that are slightly creased in the center and face each other as they grow from a circular clump, unlike the similar-looking but flat, fanlike habit of iris leaves. The six-petaled orange flowers grow on tall, leafless stalks and only open for one day. The tubers often grow just inches beneath the soil surface and are easy to collect. They resemble miniature thin-skinned potatoes about the size of a pinky finger.

Only the new, white tubers are good for eating, older ones become brown, punky, and inedible. Steam, boil, or bake the tubers until tender. (They don't need to be peeled.) You can boil and cream them, bake them, make them into fritters, or eat

them raw. The shoots, flower buds, and petals are also edible. Eat the young shoots steamed, boiled, or sautéed in oil or butter. Use the flower buds raw in salads, or boil, pickle, or stir-fry them. Dip the flowers in batter and deep-fry them tempura-style or add them to omelettes. Dried daylily flowers, called golden needles (gum-tsoy or gum-jum), are are popular ingredient in many Chinese soups and stews.

A garden plant escaped from cultivation, tawny daylily, *Hemerocallis fulva*, makes a great candidate for foraging. Don't gather tubers found growing near roadways, however: They may harbor residues from car exhaust or pesticides.

Making More Tubers

Alessandro Chiari

Nothing could be easier than increasing your supply of edible corms, tubers, and rhizomatous crops at home. That's because virtually all the delicious tubers featured in this book favor vegetative, or asexual, propagation—propagation from a part of the plant other than the seeds. Unlike propagation from seed, vegetative propagation produces plants that are identical to the mother plant, which can be an advantage if you are eager to increase your stock of attractive and tasty plants without genetic surprises. Read on to pick up a few simple techniques that will help you take full advantage of the tubers busily making duplicates of themselves underground.

Propagating Corms

Corms are short, swollen stems that grow at or below the ground. Common plants with this type of storage organ are *Colocasia, Xanthosoma,* and *Ensete*. Corms have buds that can develop either leaves and inflorescences, which grow aboveground, or new corms, which allow the plant to self-propagate asexually. Sometimes these newly formed corms are small in size; these are called cormels. In the tropical environment newly formed corms will start growing right away, producing leaves and stems that grow up in a cluster around the mother plant; they are commonly described as suckers. Plants with this type of storage organ are easy to propagate. Dig out the plant, separate the corms or cormels from the mother plant and replant them—or at least the ones you don't plan to eat. The corms and cormels of tropical plants are difficult to store, so it's a good practice to replant them right away.

Propagating Rhizomes

Rhizomes are underground fleshy stems that grow horizontally. *Canna, Helianthus tuberosus,* and *Nelumbo nucifera* are typical examples of plants that form rhizomes. Gardeners usually propagate rhizomes through division, when the plant is dormant. To do this, loosen the soil around the plant and using a garden fork, gently dig out the entire clump. If you can, pull apart the rhizomes by hand; if they are very large or too tangled to separate easily, cut the rhizomes into sections with a sharp, clean knife, making sure that each piece has at least one bud. Discard rhizomes that are brown-fleshed and mushy—they are rotten and won't regrow. Replant the divisions right away, before they have a chance to dry out. It's usually beneficial to cut short or remove large leaves or tall stems to encourage the growth of the new buds and help the newly set plant to stay anchored against the elements.

Taro, *Colocasia esculenta*, and other plants that arise from corms often form new cormels that allow the plant to self-propagate asexually. To propagate the plant, dig it out, gently separate the new corms, and replant them right away.

Seed potatoes are whole tubers, or sections of larger ones, that have at least one "eye," or bud. Each seed potato gives rise to a new plant that will in turn produce many delicious new potatoes. Eat some, share some, and save a few for planting the following spring.

Propagating Tubers

A tuber is a modified, fleshy stem that functions as an underground storage organ. The most common tuber is the potato. The "eyes" of a potato are the buds, from which new leaves and stems originate. Each eye is formed by an axillary bud and a leaf scar right below it. Given the right conditions, at the end of its dormancy period a tuber's bud will sprout and produce shoots that will eventually emerge from underground. The energy needed for sprouting and the new plant's subsequent growth is provided by the starch in the fleshy tuber.

To propagate tubers, plant the entire storage organ—or a good-sized section that contains at least one bud—when it begins sprouting. If using divisions, make sure the sections aren't too small, or the bud might not have enough energy to grow into a shoot. For potatoes, two-ounce chunks are about right. If you're using cut sections, store them at room temperature with high humidity for two or three days before planting to allow the formation of a protective callus on the surface of the cuts.

Buying Tubers

Scott D. Appell

It's wonderful fun perusing nursery catalogs and trawling the Web to find tubers to grow, harvest, and cook, and it's also likely that you'll have to rely on mail-order purchases for some of the more elusive plants portrayed in the encyclopedia. But don't forget that quite a few of the tubers in this book are easily available at greenmarkets and grocery stores. This approach is not only far less expensive but also holds the advantage of allowing you to carefully sort through the tubers on offer and choose the healthiest, freshest specimens yourself—not an option when shopping by mail. In addition—and this is perhaps the best part—in the market, you can experience something of the culture in which the tubers are part of daily life and browse among the herbs, spices, condiments, and cooking utensils traditionally used in their preparation.

Before setting out, it helps to know where to look for the tubers you plan to grow. Asian markets often stock taro (*Colocasia esculenta*), Chinese water chestnut (*Eleocharis dulcis*), Chinese arrowhead (*Sagittaria trifolia* var. *sinensis*), yam (*Dioscorea alata*), and sacred lotus (*Nelumbo nucifera*). Hispanic markets often sell yuca (*Manihot esculenta*), yautía (*Xanthosoma sagittifolium*), jícama (*Pachyrhizus erosus*), and giant taro (*Alocasia macrorrhiza*). Afro-Caribbean markets sometimes carry the fresh arrowroot tuber (*Maranta arundinacea*). Most supermarkets stock Jerusalem artichoke (*Helianthus tuberosus*) and sweet potato (*Ipomoea batatas*). They also supply potatoes (*Solanum tuberosum*), of course, but for those it's best to buy seed potatoes from certified commercially produced stock, available in spring at most nurseries and farm stores. The store-bought spuds may have been treated with a sprouting retardant, but even if they haven't, using noncertified stock puts you at risk of introducing diseases and pests (such as nematodes) to your garden.

When shopping for tubers to grow, the same rules apply as when you are shopping for tubers to eat. Always look for unblemished skin: Avoid tubers with cuts, nicks, abrasions, or scars. Also reject tubers with soft spots, black areas, or corky bits, which suggest that decay has set in. Tubers should smell earthy, not moldy—there is a difference, and you can train your nose to sense it. Largest is not always best. When shopping for jícama to eat, the small- to medium-size tubers are tastiest; similarly, when looking for tubers to plant, choose the smallest ones, which will settle in and multiply more readily than large ones. If you are scrutinizing food-market lotus rhizomes to plant, look for the bud shields (growing points), located at the tips of each section—if the shields are missing, the root cannot grow. Many Chinese markets now sell vacuum-packed lotus rhizomes, a precleaned, pretrimmed, sealed convenience food that is easier to process for the table but will never sprout. And it goes without saying that anything sold in a can will never grow.

The "Tubers at a Glance" table on the following pages provides an overview of root vegetables, tubers, rhizomes, and corms for shopping and growing.

Check the greenmarkets in your neighborhood for tubers to grow in your garden. This is both economical and entertaining, and you can choose the healthiest tubers yourself.

Tubers at a Glance

PLANT	HARDINESS ZONES	NATURAL HABITAT
Alocasia macrorrhiza Giant taro, ape*	10–11	Tropics
Amorphophallus konjac Devil's tongue, konjac	10–11	Tropics
Apios americana Groundnut	4–8	Sunny marsh
Arisaema triphyllum Jack-in-the-pulpit*	4–9	Woodland
Boesenbergia rotunda Chinese keys	8–10	Tropics
Canna edulis Edible canna	10–11	Subtropics
Claytonia virginica Spring beauty	5–9	Woodland
Colocasia esculenta Elephant's ear, taro*	9–11	Tropics
Cyperus esculentus Earth almond, tiger nut	8–11	Disturbed areas; cultivated fields
Dahlia hybrids Dahlia	9–11	Garden origin
Dioscorea alata Yam*	10–11	Tropics
Eleocharis dulcis Chinese water chestnut	10–11	Bog
Ensete ventricosum Ensete	11	Subtropics
Helianthus tuberosus Jerusalem artichoke	4–9	Woodland edge
Hemerocallis fulva Tawny daylily	3–10	Woodland edge
Ipomoea batatas Sweet potato	10–11	Subtropics
Lathyrus tuberosus Earth chestnut	6–11	Woodland edges; hedgerows

*This tuber contains alkaloids or other substances that make it unsuitable for raw consumption. Always cook before eating.

Hispanic markets	Overwinter indoors or store rhizome during its dormancy.
See Nursery Sources, page 113	Store indoors during its 4- to 5-month dormancy at 60°F–68°F.
See Nursery Sources, page 113	Perennial to Zone 4
See Nursery Sources, page 113	Perennial to Zone 4
See Nursery Sources, page 113	Overwinter indoors or store rhizome during its dormancy.
See Nursery Sources, page 113	Store rhizomes in cool, frost-free area over winter; replant in spring.
See Nursery Sources, page 113	Perennial to Zone 5
Asian markets	Remove tuber for winter storage when frost kills the tops.
Not recommended	Invasive plant. See page 99 in "Foraging for Wild Tubers."
See Nursery Sources, page 113	Bring tubers indoors over winter; replant in spring when soil is warm.
Asian markets	Grow as annual.
Asian markets	Store seed corms over winter in a cool spot; replant in spring.
See Nursery Sources, page 113	Bring inside in autumn to sunroom or greenhouse; watch for aphids and mites.
Supermarkets	Perennial to Zone 4
Not recommended	Invasive plant. See page 102 in "Foraging for Wild Tubers."
Supermarkets	Requires subtropical heat to excel.
See Nursery Sources, page 113	Sow seed outdoors in midspring.

Tubers at a Glance *continued*

PLANT	HARDINESS ZONES	NATURAL HABITAT
Manihot esculenta Cassava, manioc, yuca*	10–11	Tropics
Maranta arundinacea Arrowroot	9–11	Tropics
Nelumbo nucifera Sacred lotus	4–11	Aquatic
Oxalis tuberosa Oca*	8–11	Alpine
Pachyrhizus erosus Yam bean, jícama	10–11	Tropics
Pediomelum esculentum Prairie turnip	4–11	Prairie
Plectranthus esculentus Livingstone potato	10–11	Tropics
Sagittaria trifolia var. *sinensis* Chinese arrowhead	7–11	Swamp
Smallanthus sonchifolius Yacón	10–11	Subtropics
Solanum jamesii Colorado wild potato*	9–11	Grassland; coniferous forest
Solanum tuberosum cultivars Potato*	Annual	Cultivated to grow in many habitats
Stachys affinis Chinese artichoke, crosne	9–11	Bog
Tropaeolum tuberosum Tuberous nasturtium	3–6	Alpine
Typha latifolia Broadleaf cattail	3–11	Bog
Ullucus tuberosus Ulluco	7–10	Alpine
Xanthosoma sagittifolium Yautía*	10–11	Tropics

*This tuber contains alkaloids or other substances that make it unsuitable for raw consumption. Always cook before eating.

WHERE TO BUY	IN NORTHERN GARDENS
Hispanic markets	Summer outdoors in pot; bring into greenhouse or bay window over winter.
See Nursery Sources, page 113	Requires very high humidity; grow in greenhouse.
Asian markets	Perennial to Zone 4
See Nursery Sources, page 113	Store tubers over winter in damp sand; replant in spring or grow in alpine house.
Hispanic markets	Plant small tubers in spring; southern gardeners may have success growing from seed.
See Nursery Sources, page 113	Perennial to Zone 4
See Nursery Sources, page 113	Summer outdoors in pot; bring into greenhouse or bay window over winter.
Asian markets	Store corms in damp sand over winter; replant in spring after last frost.
See Nursery Sources, page 113	Grow as an annual or store tubers in damp peat moss for spring replanting.
See Nursery Sources, page 113	Harvest tubers after frost kills top growth; store in cool spot and replant in spring.
Supermarkets	Plant when soil warms; harvest in late summer or early fall.
See Nursery Sources, page 113	Harvest after frost kills top growth; store tubers over winter and replant in spring.
See Nursery Sources, page 113	Grow as annual.
See Nursery Sources, page 113	Perennial to Zone 3
See Nursery Sources, page 113	Grow in pot as a cold alpine plant.
Hispanic markets	Grow in large container; repot often to accommodate plant's growth.

For More Information

BOTANICAL, ETHNOBOTANICAL, AND HORTICULTURAL BOOKS

Andean Roots and Tubers
Michael Hermann and J. Heller, eds.
International Plant Genetics Research
Institute, 1997

Aroids: Plants of the Arum Family
Deni Bown
Timber Press, 2000

The Cambridge World History of Food
Kenneth F. Kiple
Cambridge University Press, 2000

*The Cassava Transformation: Africa's Best
Kept Secret*
F.I. Nweke, D.S.C. Spenser, and J.K. Lynam
Michigan State University Press, 2002

Crops and Man
Jack R. Harlan
American Society of Agronomy, 1992

*Foraging and Farming: The Evolution of
Plant Exploitation*
David R. Harris and Gordon C. Hillman, eds.
Unwin Hyman, 1989

The History and Social Influence of the Potato
Redcliffe Salaman (J.K. Hawkes, ed.)
Cambridge University Press, 1985

Native American Ethnobotany
Daniel E. Moerman
Timber Press, 1998

Notes of a Potato Watcher
James J. Lang
Texas A&M University Press, 2001

*Potato: The Definitive Guide to Potatoes and
Potato Cooking*
Alex Barker and Sallie Mansfield
Lorenz Books, 1999

*The Potato: How the Humble Spud Rescued
the Western World*
Larry Zukerman
Faber and Faber, 1998

FORAGING GUIDES AND CULINARY BOOKS

Cornucopia II: A Source Book of Edible Plants
Stephen Facciola
Kampong Publications, 1998

Food Plants of the World: An Illustrated Guide
Ben-Erik Van Wyk
Timber Press, 2005

*The Forager's Harvest: A Guide to Identifying,
Harvesting and Preparing Edible Wild Plants*
Samuel Thayer
Forager's Harvest Press, 2006

Gourmet Cooking for Free
Bradford Angier
Willow Creek Press, 1970

*Plants for a Future: Edible & Useful Plants
for a Healthier World*
Ken Fern
Permanent Publications, 1997

Stalking the Wild Asparagus.
Euell Gibbons
David McKay Co., 1962

*Wild Roots: A Forager's Guide to the Edible &
Medicinal Roots, Tubers, Corms & Rhizomes
of North America*
Douglas B. Elliott
Inner Traditions International, 1995

*Recipes from La Isla! New & Traditional
Puerto Rican Cuisine*
Robert Rosado and Judith Healy Rosado
Lowell House, 1995

WEBSITES

www.bioversityinternational.org/Plants_and_
Animals/Roots_Tubers_and_Aroids
Bioversity International: Roots, Tubers, and
Aroids

www.cipotato.org
International Potato Center

www.plants.usda.gov
USDA Natural Resources Conservation
Service PLANTS Database

Nursery Sources

The Banana Tree (jícama)
715 Northampton Street
Easton, PA 18042
610-253-9589
www.banana-tree.com
(catalog $3)

Companion Plants (cattail)
7247 North Coolidge Ridge Road
Athens, Ohio 45701
614-592-4643
www.companionplants.com

Ernst Conservation Seeds (earth chestnut)
9006 Mercer Pike
Meadville, PA 16335
800-873-3321
www.ernstseed.com

Fraser's Thimble Farms (jack-in-the-pulpit)
175 Arbutus Road
Salt Spring Island, V8K 1A3 B.C.
Canada
Fax: 250-537-5788
www.thimblefarms.com
(mail and fax orders only)

Gardens of the Blue Ridge (spring beauty)
P.O. Box 10
Pineola, NC 28604
704-733-2417
www.gardensoftheblueridge.com

GingersRus (Chinese keys)
www.gingersrus.com

Irish Eyes & Garden City Seeds (potatoes)
P.O. Box 307
Thorp, WA 98946
509-964-7000
www.Irish-eyes.com

J.L. Hudson, Seedsman (yams, devil's tongue)
Star Route 2, Box 337
La Honda, CA 94020
www.jlhudsonseeds.com
(catalog $1)

Ronniger Potato Farm (potatoes, Jerusalem artichoke)
HCR 62, Box 332A
Moyie Springs, ID 83845
208-267-7938
www.ronnigers.com

Nichols Garden Nursery (yacón)
1190 Old Salem Road N.E.
Albany, OR 97321
800-422-3985
www.nicholsgardennursery.com

Milk Ranch Specialty Potatoes (potatoes)
20094 Highway 149
Powderhorn, CO 81243
970-641-5634
www.milkranch.com

Plant Delights Nursery (edible aroids)
9241 Sauls Road
Raleigh, NC 27603
919-722-4794
www.plantdelights.com

Prairie Moon Nursery (prairie turnip)
31837 Bur Oak Lane
Winona, MN 55987-9515
866-417-8156
www.prairiemoon.com

Thompson & Morgan Seedsmen (enset)
P.O. Box 1308
Jackson, NJ 08527-0308
www.thompson-morgan.com

Trade Winds Fruit (Chinese water chestnut, arrowroot)
P.O. Box 232693
Encinitas, CA 92023
www.tradewindsfruit.com

Tropilab (yuca, yams, arrowroot)
6428 18th Avenue North
St. Petersburg, FL 33710-5528
727-344-7608
www.tropilab.com

Contributors

Scott D. Appell is a regular contributor to BBG publications. He has edited the handbooks *Annuals for Every Garden* (2003), *The Potted Garden* (2001), and *Landscaping Indoors* (2000) and is a frequent contributor to BBG's award-winning *Plants & Gardens News*. He is also the author of four books; *Pansies*, *Lilies*, *Tulips*, and *Orchids*. He lives, writes, gardens, and teaches horticulture on the island of Vieques, Puerto Rico.

Alessandro Chiari has been the plant propagator at Brooklyn Botanic Garden since 1998. He studied tropical agriculture at the University of Florence, Italy, and plant science at the University of Connecticut, and he has worked as a horticulturist in Zambia, Paraguay, Chile, and Peru.

Beth Hanson is a former managing editor of Brooklyn Botanic Garden's handbook series and is editor of nine BBG handbooks, including *Designing an Herb Garden* (2004), *Natural Disease Control* (2000), *Chile Peppers* (1999), and *Easy Compost* (1997). She also contributed to *The Brooklyn Botanic Garden's Gardener's Desk Reference* (Henry Holt, 1998). She lives outside New York City and writes about gardening, health, and the environment for various publications.

James J. Lang is an associate professor of sociology and former director of the Center for Latin American and Iberian Studies at Vanderbilt University. He has done fieldwork on basic food crops in Latin America, Asia, and Africa. His recent books include *Notes of a Potato Watcher*, a story of cultivated potatoes and how they spread as a staple throughout the world, and *Feeding a Hungry Planet*, about rice production and the green revolution.

Leda Meredith teaches gardening and botany classes at Brooklyn Botanic Garden and at the New York Botanical Garden. She holds a certificate in ethnobotany from the New York Botanical Garden and is also an adjunct professor at Adelphi University. She is a professional gardener with both commercial and residential clients and leads wild edible plant walks in the New York City area. Her writing has appeared in *The Herb Companion*, *Pointe Magazine*, *The Vu*, and other publications.

Photos

Dave Allen page 35

John Bamberg page 71 bottom

David Cavagnaro cover, pages 5, 6 and back cover, 11, 13, 15, 16, 18, 19, 20 and back cover, 24, 27 (2), 29, 33 top, 34 and back cover, 37, 38, 39, 45, 46, 49, 53 (2), 59 bottom, 68, 72, 73, 76, 77, 83, 92, 95, 98, 101, 102, 105

Mark Czarnota, University of Georgia, www.insectimages.org page 99

Alan & Linda Detrick pages 14, 28

Liza Donatelli pages 7, 43, 57, 84, 86, 89, 91, 107

Jonas Fansa page 31

Derek Fell pages 8, 10, 23, 41, 42, 59 top, 60, 67 top

Josef Hlasek page 50

Steve Hurst, USDA-NRCS Plants Database page 51

International Potato Center pages 12, 80 (2), 81

Tomas Kubicek page 25

Charles Marden Fitch pages 47, 67 bottom, 104

Ralf Omlor page 69

Jerry Pavia pages 2, 17, 56, 75, 79

José Maria Sanchez de Lorenzo-Cáceres page 54

James R. Sime page 63

T. Tolbert, Escalante BLM (contributed by U.S. Potato Genebank, Sturgeon Bay, WI) page 71 top

Ben-Erik van Wyk pages 30 (2), 33 bottom, 64, 65

Index

PROVIDING EXPERT GARDENING ADVICE FOR OVER 60 YEARS

Join Brooklyn Botanic Garden as an annual Subscriber Member and receive our next three gardening handbooks delivered directly to you, plus *Plants & Gardens News*, *BBG Members News*, and reciprocal privileges at many botanic gardens across the country. Visit bbg.org/subscribe for details.

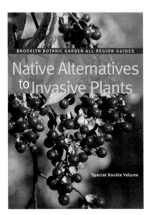

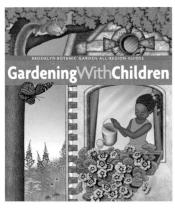

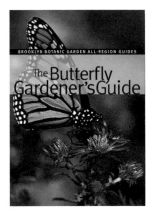

BROOKLYN BOTANIC GARDEN ALL-REGION GUIDES

World renowned for pioneering gardening information, Brooklyn Botanic Garden's award-winning guides provide practical advice in a compact format for gardeners in every region of North America. To order other fine titles, call 718-623-7286 or shop online at shop.bbg.org. For additional information about Brooklyn Botanic Garden, call 718-623-7200 or visit bbg.org.